Love ta Junelle and Best wishes

Hope you like this version better than the other.

Charles Richard Drew

Sprinter in Life

from
Aunt Dorothy Rosenberg
a.k.a. Dorothy Young Croman

This book is being put into the New York State curriculum for Jr. High Schools.

Dorothy Young Croman

April 5, 1992.

"TO SOW THE FALLOW SOIL"

PENNYWELL DRIVE . P.O. BOX 90883 . NASHVILLE, TENNESSEE 37209

WINSTON-DEREK
Publishers, Inc.

First printing 1988

Second printing 1992

PUBLISHED BY WINSTON-DEREK PUBLISHERS, INC.
Nashville, Tennessee 37205

Library of Congress Catalog Card No: 87-42904
ISBN: 1-55523-113-6

Printed in the United States of America

To the betterment of African-Americans

We were extremely fortunate in that the best trained physician of our group, Charles Richard Drew, elected to prepare others in his chosen field of surgery. He was precociously paternalistic, a very rare characteristic of men of medicine. He exhibited the Christian attitude of returning good for evil and got a great kick out of serving and bringing recognition and glory to the Howard University College of Medicine, the school that rejected him.

C. Herbert Marshall, M.D.
former president, National Medical Association

CONTENTS

Foreword   ix

Preface   xiii

Acknowledgements   xv

1. Working and Playing Together   1

2. The Newspaper Business   7

3. The End of World War I   11

4. Sister Elsie Dies   17

5. Charlie Learns to Study   21

6. An Athletic Scholarship to Amherst   25

7. A New World to Conquer   29

8. Discrimination Rears Its Ugly Head   33

9. Charlie Becomes Coach at Morgan   39

10. A Desire to Study Medicine   43

11. McGill University: 1929   47

12. Charlie's Father Dies   53

13. A Rockefeller Foundation Fellowship   57

14. Columbia University: 1938   61

15. Lenore Robbins Enters His Life   65

16. Blood for Britain   69

17. Drew Becomes Medical Supervisor   75

18. Perfecting Blood Plasma   81

19. "Let Him Die!"   85

20. A Return to Howard University   87

21. "Bloods Are No Longer Separated"   93

22. Serving as a Trustee on Many Boards   99

23. Dr. Drew Dies Tragically in 1950   103

    Epilogue   107

FOREWORD

(The following was taken from an article in Phylon *in 1950.)*

Many honors came to Dr. Charles Richard Drew before his untimely death in 1950, and many more were given afterwards.

This outstanding man and physician-surgeon who would have such an impact in the field of blood and blood plasma— and on the lives of many a young surgeon—started making his mark while still in college at Amherst.

Students, teachers, and colleagues held him in high esteem and respect, as the following comments assert.

Guichard Parris, former classmate of Dr. Drew and Director of Public Relations for the National Urban League in New York City, had this to say, on December 12, 1966, about his friend, ". . . Dr. Drew was a man of action. But he was also a man who was greatly interested in scholarly pursuits. He had a sense of social responsibility and showed this very outstandingly at Amherst. He befriended the underdog. At the Howard School of Medicine, he was well known for his great interest in the training of the future men of medicine and surgery. I considered him to be a warm friend."

Reports from Amherst College were interesting, although there was nothing at that time to foreshadow Dr. Drew's later brilliant medical career.

In the *Amherst Alumni News* of May 1950 is an article entitled "Charles Richard Drew, '26," written by Newton F. McKeon, which says in part, ". . . No account of his Amherst days is complete without some estimate of the regard in which he was held by his fellows. He was frank, direct, soft-spoken, with good nature showing in both face and manner. He had a high degree of natural dignity unalloyed by vanity. He had his reticences and clearly possessed his own self respect. With these qualities he had the respect, the esteem, and the affectionate admiration of his classmates and contemporaries."

The annual yearbook, *Olio*, with an item about Charlie Drew in his junior year, indicates further the affection and respect in which he was held: "Yes, this is Charlie Drew about whom you have heard so much, the terror of football opponents, the young ladies' delight, and the frank, straightforward lad in whom all mothers put their trust. Charlie's good nature is known wherever he is known, and that is over a rather extensive area, vouch the Post Office clerks. Like a knight of old is our hero. His straight arm is the trusty lance that has battered the helm of many a foe. His ukulele is the melodious harp whose sweet notes, accompanied by his own caroling, conquer the stoniest heart. And Lizzie is the fleet steed which carries its knightly master in search of nightly adventure."

Dr. Harold H. Plough, Professor Emeritus of Amherst College, on December 2, 1966 wrote, "I remember Charlie Drew well during his college days on this campus. He was a popular, soft-spoken, handsome young man, best known as an outstanding athlete. He excelled in football as a halfback, and in track events as a quarter miler. In those days it was inevitable that he should be somewhat idolized by his fellow students, and that any intellectual qualities should be minimized. He was friendly with other students, and often a favored companion because he played the guitar. I seem to remember that he worked with the Amherst Boys Club. Altogether he was a strong, friendly, cooperative member of the college community . . . I remember him as a member of my sophomore biology class. He was a quiet, reliable student, who made a good but not outstanding record. Unlike the majority, he showed a special interest in the laboratory work in which he did especially good work. Perhaps this was a suggestive forerunner of his later interest in surgery. . . (otherwise) Dr. Drew's outstanding contributions to medical science and medical education did not appear to be foreshadowed during his Amherst days."

Dr. E. H. Bensley, Vice-Dean, Faculty of Medicine of McGill University, Montreal, Canada, in a letter dated October 11, 1966 said, "He (Charles Richard Drew) maintained an excellent academic record throughout the five years of his medical course, was elected a member of the Alpha Omega Alpha Honour Medical Society, of which he became vice-president, and in his final year at McGill was awarded the J. Francis Williams Fellowship in Medicine, described as one of the highest honours open to senior students. . . . He was active in the Medical Undergraduate Society and also played a prominent role in the world of the *McGill Medical Journal*, the official publication of that Society."

On Monday, April 10,1950, Senator Hubert H. Humphrey, of the 81st Congress of the United States, asked and obtained leave to have printed in the *Congressional Record—Senate*, an editorial from the *Washington Post* of April 6,1950, in tribute to the late Dr. Charles R. Drew, and an obituary notice of his death from the *New York Times* of April 2, 1950.

No greater tribute was ever given any man, regardless of race, creed, or national origin.

PAUL B. CORNELY

PREFACE

In 1954 I began working for the public schools in Seattle, Washington. It was the beginning of our racial problems due to the integration decision by the Supreme Court. I worked in the secretarial office.

Our manager was a delightful young black woman who went out of her way to help me understand what the issue of race was all about. This was my first contact with minorities, and I was not familiar with racial problems.

Another friend of mine, a charming black social worker, became sympathetic with my desire to explore racial issues through my writing. Since I write mainly for young children, I wondered how this skill could be used to its best advantage.

A third friend who encouraged me was a small, vivacious white woman, the social worker in charge of the staff of social workers for the Seattle schools.

Then I began to hear about the black doctor Charles Richard Drew and his outstanding blood plasma research, which had helped the blood for Britain project during World War II. In 1950 he had been fatally injured in a car accident. I became interested in the questions as to what kind of care he received before he died and the false rumors that were started. I decided his life story would be a good example for young people and thought that perhaps at the same time, I could put an end to hearsay. My friends encouraged me to write about him.

DOROTHY YOUNG CROMAN

ACKNOWLEDGMENTS

Thank you, Mamie Franklin Price, Mildred German, and Amorette Richards. What wonderful support you have all given me over the years. I faltered many times, but my book for older children is now a reality.

I want to give special thanks to the Drew families for their help and cooperation—Mrs. Charles Richard Drew and Dr. Drew's sisters and brother: Mrs. Francis Gregory of Washington, D.C.; Mrs. John Pennington of St. Albany, New York; and Mr. Joseph L. Drew of Arlington, Virginia.

Also, to Mrs. Dorothy Porter, head librarian of the Moorland Room, Founders Library, Howard University, and Miss Betty Jo Lanier, her assistant; Miss Georgia Cowan, head biographer, and Miss Arlene Jackson, both of the district of Columbia Central Library; Mrs. Margaret Powell, head librarian, and Mrs. Geraldine Hurt, of the Mt. Pleasant Branch; and the Library of Congress.

To Mr. Robert Watkins, Public Relations Department of Freedmen's Hospital; Mr. G. Frederick Stanton, secretary of Howard University, and Mr. Charles H. Bush, supervisor of off-campus housing; Mr. William R. Breyer, Office of Public Information, American Red Cross; Mrs. Beatrice M. Reed, all of Washington, D.C.

To the Medical Library of the University of Washington, Seattle, Washington.

Last, but not least, to Dr. J. W. Nabrit, Jr., past president of Howard University, who earlier helped me get in touch with Mrs. Charles R. Drew in order to start work on this children's biography.

I have been asked my opinion of the practice
of separating the blood of Caucasian and Negro donors.
My opinion is not important. The fact is that
test by race does not stand up in the laboratory.

Charles Richard Drew, M.D., C.M., ScB.

One

Working and Playing Together

"CHARLIE WINS!! CHARLIE WINS! Charlie Drew wins!"

The cries were loud in Charlie's ears as he touched the side of the pool. He jerked the water out of his eyes and looked up. The young pool manager, muscular and black, was trying to keep people back. Kids—black and brown, fat and skinny—were jumping up and down, screaming.

Charlie reached up and grasped the edge to pull himself out. A firm freckled hand reached down to help.

Charlie grinned. "Hi, Pop." He gave a heave as Pop pulled, and soon he was standing, his head reaching to his father's shoulder.

They stood out as different from the others. Pop's hair was a bushy red. Right now Charlie's was a slicked-down brown and dripping wet. Neither father nor son was black- or brown-skinned, but red and freckled.

"You did all right, son! You did all right! Mighty proud, I am!" Mr. Drew hugged Charlie and didn't care if his clothes did get wet. Then his mom, carrying baby Nora, was there, with Elsie and Joe tagging along. She kissed Charlie but did not want any water spattered on the baby, who was not yet a month old.

"I knew you could do it! I knew you could! Get dressed and we'll eat. I have a picnic lunch all ready. You'll get lots of fried chicken today!" She turned to herd her little group back toward the huge picnic basket that sat to one side.

Just then the young manager grabbed Charlie's arm and raised it high.

"The winner!" he shouted. "Here's the medal for the winner!" He held it up so the crowd could see.

"Yay! Yay! Yay!" The shouts became louder.

He pinned the small swimming medal on the wet shoulder strap of Charlie's black swim suit and shook his hand.

"Congratulations, young Charlie! You've officially opened our new Mott Swimming Pool in our first meet. May you win many more!"

"Th-thanks!" stammered Charlie. He had not expected this. It made him feel silly.

Pop tried to pull him toward the edge of the crowd, but people kept grabbing him. He kept saying, "Thank you," as he knew his mom would want, but winning surely had its drawbacks. He did not like all this fuss. Anyway, now he was hungry. He had not eaten earlier.

That hot summer day in June gave Charles Richard Drew his first swimming medal, just before his ninth birthday. He would have three more medals before the summer was over. Today's meet had been special because it was the first one held in the first outdoor pool for blacks, across from Mott School in Washington, D.C. Fair-skinned Charlie Drew was one of the best neighborhood swimmers. He wanted mightily to become the best. He and his friends, Bill Hastie among them, had many close matches.

The neighborhood in which the Drew family lived was called Foggy Bottom because of the heavy mists from the Potomac River. Much of the area was filled in, but there were many mosquitoes, which caused malaria. If Mr. and Mrs. Richard Drew felt that another part of the city would be more healthy, nothing much was said. They lived where Negroes were allowed to live.

Charlie was born on Friday, June 3, 1904, in Grandmother and Grandfather Drew's home, on 21st Street near Elm. Grandma Drew was a firm, determined woman, not much given to viewing the lighter side of life, but Grandpa Drew was fun-loving. He liked to play jokes, and Charlie, mischievous and full of pranks, was like him, even down to his long, slender fingers. When excited, he talked as much with his hands as with his mouth.

Later the family moved into the home of Grandmother and Grandfather Burrell on 18th Street. It was there that two of Charlie's sisters, Elsie and Nora, and his brother Joe were born. Rawlins Park, directly across the street, was a wonderful playground. The children spent hours climbing the fragrant pink magnolia trees.

Grandfather Burrell, called Grandpa Joe, a dogcatcher by trade, raised a few chickens, and this gave the family plenty of eggs, as well as chicken for a tasty dish on the table.

Emma, Mrs. Drew's younger sister, better known as Midge, was also part of the family at that time. She and Elsie and Charlie all attended Stevens Elementary School. When Midge, six months older than Charlie, wanted to put him in his place, she'd say firmly, "Remember! *I* am your Aunt Emma! Please call me that!"

His only response was to play another joke on her.

The family enjoyed doing things together. Picnics, swimming, Sunday-afternoon band concerts—all free—gave many hours of pleasure.

They almost wore out the old victrola with their favorite Caruso records. Pop played the guitar and sang baritone while Mom sang alto. The children loved to join in such songs as:

> Reuben, Reuben, I've been thinking
> what a queer world this would be,
> If the men were all transported
> far beyond the Northern Sea . . . .

The verses went on and on. When the neighbors were in one of the family songfests, no one knew when to stop.

Mr. and Mrs. Drew sang in the church choir, and Mr. Drew also directed the junior choir, using a long yellow pencil for his baton. He turned out some fine singers.

One time Pop, for some reason, decided to shave off his mustache. Charlie heard him tell Mom that he was tired of it and needed a change.

3

"You won't like it," she warned. "You've had it too long. I don't think I'd like you without it, either."

Charlie was sure her brown eyes were twinkling; he could hear the chuckle in her voice.

"We'll see," responded Pop. "We'll see."

Nothing more was said, so Charlie forgot about it.

Then one Sunday morning a new face appeared in the choir. Charlie took a second look. Why, it was Pop! Without his mustache! It didn't look like Pop, but it must be! He had the same bushy red hair.

At that moment Joe, sitting next to Charlie, poked him. "Who's the new man up there?"

"It's Pop, you nut!" muttered Charlie, under cover of the singing.

"Pop!?" Joe's voice rose shrilly.

"Yes! Pop! Shut up!"

Stern looks from both parents finally quieted Joe, but all through the service Charlie could hear him giggling softly from time to time.

Pop soon let his mustache grow in again. Mom had been right. His smooth face wasn't the success he had hoped.

Mr. Drew was a good father. He supported his family with his job as carpet layer and upholsterer, and also enjoyed helping the neighborhood children with any projects they might have. He was an excellent swimmer, and he taught more than one child to swim well.

Mrs. Drew could swim too, but she did not have the same interest. She did worry while special races were going on. Once during a tub race, she became excited when Charlie's tub turned over and he failed to come up immediately.

When Charlie had felt himself tipping over, he dived to get away from the tub. He had not realized he was staying down so long, and when he popped up, he saw Mom at the edge of the pool, ready to jump in to save him. They all had a good laugh over that.

Elsie was not as active as the other children. Sometimes Charlie could hear their parents talking, wondering if she were well. They decided it was just a "phase" she would outgrow. It did not occur to any member of the family that her trouble might be serious.

4

Both parents felt strongly that families should work and play together and that children should study hard. In the evenings, after the dishes were done, Mom would say, "Time for study, everyone!" in a quiet but firm voice, and she would pull the gas lamp with its brightly colored porcelain shade down from the high ceiling. Then the children knew it was time to be quiet.

Lamplight brought out glints of highlights on the shining heads bent so industriously. Elsie and Charlie had brown hair, with the skin coloring of their father; they turned red in the sun, as he did, and freckled. But Joe and Nora had the fair complexion and brown eyes of their mother.

Mom even taught her sons to dance. She insisted that the more social graces children knew, the better they would get along in the world. Sometimes the boys were not sure they wanted to know this part of the world, but they went along good-naturedly.

The children also learned about discrimination and some of the hardships it caused. They learned which places they could enter and which they could not. It was simply a way of life, and they accepted it. But they had a good life, and neither parent felt the children would suffer unduly if they could learn to accept the restrictions.

If at times the parents themselves felt the unfairness of the so-called "separate but equal" facilities and opportunities, they tried not to let their feelings show. They always made their home comfortable and kept up their church work. The outside world was not too important while the children were young, but church was. Their Baptist religion was an essential part of their lives.

Two

The Newspaper Business

ALL THE DREW CHILDREN EARNED MONEY whenever and wherever they could. Charlie, being the oldest, was the first to do so. War in Europe started in 1914, when the Austrian archduke Ferdinand was murdered. First one European country and then another declared war against Germany.

During this time Charlie had been building up a good newspaper business, and on Friday, April 6, 1917, Charlie, now almost thirteen, found the paper of special interest. Having his own business gave him a chance to check the latest news before anyone else.

Today the headline was W A R in huge letters across the front page of the *Evening Star*. The morning paper had come out too early for this latest news.

The United States had entered World War I! President Wilson had no longer been able to hold to his neutral policy. Although few people wanted any part of this war in Europe, many felt the United States should have been in it long before. Too many American ships had already been sunk by German U-boats, and feelings were running high.

Charlie had heard his parents and neighbors discuss the possibility of entering the war and how it would affect members of their families. Pop would not have to go to war because he was too old, and besides, he had a family to support. Some uncles and older cousins might have to go.

A few black people felt this was one way to show their loyalty. After all, the United States was *their* country too. Many older Negroes, however, were not sure. Some, as young men, had fought in the Ninth and Tenth Cavalry divisions with Teddy Roosevelt's Rough Riders in Cuba.

"White people hold us back, then say we aren't as good as they are," said one old man, a neighbor. "I fought once. Wasn't any better off afterward."

"Wonder who'd do their work for them if we weren't around," said another. "But we still can't get a decent education without working a lot harder for it. 'Separate but equal'!" he snorted.

"No, I wouldn't fight again and spill my blood, only to be kicked off the sidewalk at home," still another spoke up. "Who plows the ground, plants the seed, harvests the crops, and builds the fine homes for white people?"

"Hush," Mrs. Drew broke in. "That's no way to talk. We have to be so good we won't be held back. Some day—I hope not too far off—all children, black and white, will learn from the same books in the same schools. But in the meantime—"

A neighbor woman interrupted. "Mrs. Drew, you don't work outside your home. Your husband earns enough for your family so you don't have to work."

Mom nodded. "That's true. I *am* fortunate."

"I have to work. I have a college education just as you do," said the woman. "But you know where I work—as a maid! I can't go through the front door in that home! I have to go through the back. I could teach school—if I could get into any school to teach. I like children, both colored and white."

Charlie remembered that Mom's face had become sad. She had no answer for that.

Some very old men remembered fighting during the Civil War, and how Negroes had been treated afterward. They just shook their heads.

Charlie was uncertain how he stood on the matter of war, except to know he was much too young to be accepted. As he stood looking at the newspaper in his hand, he wished he *were* old enough. He'd like to go over and show the enemy how well *he* could fight!

8

Charlie turned to see how the other boys were taking it. He had eight boys working for him now, including his little brother Joe. Although Joe was young, he showed promise of the same initiative and friendliness his older brother possessed.

Maybe today the boys would need more than the usual two thousand papers. Since the Munitions Building had been going up, many of the workers were so interested in the progress of the war, they would buy both the *Evening Star and* the morning *Times-Herald.* Yes, with this declaration of war, business should be brisk.

Some of the older boys were staring at the headlines, but smaller boys like Joe weren't paying much attention.

Charlie gave a shout. "Hey, you guys! Come over here!"

He waited until the boys were all near the big piles of newspapers.

"See this!?" He held up a paper with the bold headline. "All you need to do is shout, 'War! War declared!' and you'll sell every paper you have. Don't mention another thing. Get it?"

The boys "got it." Each took 150 to 200 papers to his own corner, and soon the cries of *"Star! Evening Star!* Read all about the war! United States at war with Germany!" could be heard.

They sold out within the first hour. Charlie had to order more papers twice. Tips were plentiful, mainly because people were so upset or excited over the thought of war, they did not think about change or bother to wait.

No one sold more papers that day than Charlie himself. He never missed any possibility of making a few extra cents—or dollars.

Before long he found another way to make money. When parades were held to raise money for the war effort, Charlie would get a working permit to sell peanuts. He could usually outsell most other boys; people liked his vigor and vitality, his winning smile and easy friendliness.

Charlie put some of his money into War Stamps. It was hard to save much; there were always so many places to put money. With his growing family and higher expenses, what Pop made went for basic things such as food and clothing. Not much was left for extras.

As Charlie grew older, he found it harder to take time to swim. But sometimes for relaxation, he and the other fellows

9

would hike or walk to Three Sisters Islands on the Potomac River. It was most fun to hop a freight train at 29th and K. This was always a bit of an adventure because of the danger of being caught by guards and thrown off.

The pool near the Mott School had been fine while he was small, but the bigger boys liked the river because there was more room. Also, a few large trees hung over the water in such a way that, with a rope flung up over a big branch, they could swing out fifteen or twenty feet before dropping into the water. It was great fun to see who could go farthest out before dropping with a huge splash.

Another activity began to interest Charlie—jumping. He watched some of the older high school boys high jumping and broad jumping, and he began to practice to see how far *he* could jump. This gave him a special thrill he had not felt before.

It was something to think about doing when he entered high school.

Three

The End of World War I

IN THE SPRING OF 1918 Charlie and Emma graduated from
Stevens Elementary School. Charlie's grades were only aver-
age since he did not particularly like to study.

He knew Mom and Pop wanted him to go on to college. He
himself did not think much about it because he still had four
years of high school ahead. But going on meant he could enter
all kinds of sports competition. He *would* like that!

Before Charlie entered Dunbar High School in September,
he turned his newspaper business over to Joe, because he
intended to go out for every sport Dunbar offered. Joe was still
pretty young, but he was becoming as much of a go-getter as
his older brother.

Dunbar High School, named for the Negro poet Paul
Lawrence Dunbar, was becoming known for its unusually high
scholastic standards. Many well-trained Negro teachers who
could not find positions elsewhere were coming to Dunbar.
Students, possibly the unwilling recipients of this excellent
training and teaching, often had to study much harder than
they had anticipated.

Also, Charlie forgot to reckon with his mother, who would
see that he studied. He might not be seriously thinking of college, but she was. He continued to work at whatever he could

find to help with expenses. He often delivered Special Delivery letters, which paid better than selling newspapers.

Many evenings were spent in study sessions around the big dining room table with the gas lamp pulled down from the ceiling.

"What you children learn now, what you have in your heads, can never be taken from you," said Mom, her eyes snapping.

Pop agreed. "Good habits formed in childhood are mighty important."

It was not all work or study. Often on a Friday evening or Saturday or Sunday, if they were caught up on their studies, Pop would get out his guitar, strum a bit, and the entire family would break into song. Charlie, too, liked to play, and his long, slender fingers could make the guitar fairly sing.

Pop and Mom, with their usual baritone and alto; the girls, soprano; and the boys, with their breaking voices singing anything they could, made up an enjoyable group. Sometimes a neighbor or two would drop in. The Drews were fun to be with. Pop also became well known as a folk singer. He and three friends often sang barbershop harmony on the riverboats during the summers. After his voice changed, Charlie sang baritone like his father. Years later he took up the saxophone, and Nora became an excellent pianist.

During his first fall in high school, Charlie often helped Joe figure his daily profits from the sale of the newspapers. Charlie sat in the big old Morris chair, the shiny rubber plant in its big flowerpot nearby, and he and Joe carefully counted the money each day. Sometimes profits were good; sometimes they were not. Many papers had to be sold at two or three cents each in order to make a profit. Joe learned that honesty paid.

He also learned to keep good records. An accounting had to be made to the companies that supplied the papers, since they wanted to know what had been sold and what had not. At times it bothered Joe that Charlie insisted upon being so exact. He had yet to learn that the older boy was a well-organized, precise person.

Pop encouraged Joe when he took over the newspaper business. He too stressed that doing a good job was a mighty important lesson in the world of business.

12

Charlie learned early that putting things in their places saved time. As he grew older he found he could accomplish a great deal by thinking ahead. In high school this applied mainly to sports and sports equipment, but he used this ability to advantage later, all through his busy life.

During Charlie's first year at Dunbar High, the war ended. On November 10, 1918, the family arose as usual and had their customary morning prayers. This Sunday morning their breakfast was the delicious fresh bluefish which Mr. Drew had brought in earlier from the municipal fish wharf. Often breakfast consisted of kidney stew, with newly baked rolls. After church, as they were finishing their regular Sunday dinner of roast beef, a knock was heard at the door. Hardly waiting for an invitation, a neighbor woman rushed in, wildly waving a newspaper.

"Did you hear? The war's over! It's ended! There're Extras out all about it!" She had two sons fighting "over there." Now they could come home. She began to cry.

The Drews had not yet heard, so there was great rejoicing. They were happy for this neighbor and for all parents whose sons were fighting.

During the excitement, Charlie saw Joe rush out of the house. Probably he had gone to see about selling Extras, even though it was Sunday. Mom would not like that!

Charlie himself left a short time later to be with some of his own friends. When he returned for supper, Joe had not yet come in. Actually, Charlie did not see him until Monday evening, when he was getting cleaned up after football practice. Mom was stirring some of her beef stew made from the Sunday's leftover roast; it simmered with a tantalizing aroma.

Mom, tendrils of black hair curling around her face flushed from bending over the big kettle, turned around as Joe staggered into the kitchen. He seemed to be bulging in spots. Mom's big mixing spoon dropped with a clatter.

"Joe! What's the matter? Are you hurt?"

Joe shook his head and reached into one of his pockets. "Not hurt, Mom! Just rich! Look!"

Disregarding the dishes set for supper, he started throwing handful after handful of coins on the table. Nickels and dimes and quarters began piling up. Some of the coins rolled off onto the floor. Joe ignored them and kept emptying his pockets.

By now other members of the family were gathering and asking questions. Money like this was not seen every day. How in the world had Joe obtained so much? And where?

Nora and Midge were picking up the coins that had fallen to the floor.

Joe said, "You can keep those. I have plenty more."

Pop came in. He stared at the growing pile of money. "I'll say you have plenty!" His voice became stern. "All right, Joe, where'd you get it?"

When Pop used that tone of voice, the children knew he was serious. They had better not play their game of not knowing what he meant.

"Selling papers," Joe answered promptly. Then he noticed the look on Pop's face. "Honest!" His head bobbed up and down. "Selling papers! Most of this's from tips."

"Tips!" Mom's voice rose. "You don't make tips like this just selling newspapers. Richard—" She turned toward Pop and started to say something else when Charlie remembered how it had been when the war started. He held up his hand. "Wait, Mom! It *could* be tips."

Pop said, "*Some* tips, maybe, but not *this* many!" He waved an arm toward the table, now almost covered with coins.

Charlie looked at his younger brother. "All right, Joe, how'd it happen? Pop's right! Tips were good when the war started, but not *this* good!" His clenched fist hit the table.

"I don't know," Joe admitted, frowning. "The first time a guy walked off without his change, I thought he'd made a mistake. He'd given me a quarter. I heard him say, 'So the war's over at last.'"

Joe took a big breath. Pop started to say something, then stopped as Joe continued. "I followed him and kept pulling at his arm. 'Here's your change, Mister,' I kept saying. 'Hey, Mister, here's your change!' I thought he was deaf or something. Finally he looked at me and said, 'Change? Oh, keep it!' and he just walked on. Then other guys came along and grabbed papers. Nobody waited for change!"

Joe looked first at Mom and then at Pop. "What *could* I do? I *did* try to give it back!" He seemed close to tears.

14

"All right," said Pop. His sternness had vanished. He sensed that Joe was telling the truth. "I guess you did all you could."

Mom sighed and turned toward the stove. "War does strange things to people," she said softly. Then, not so softly, "Please get that money off the table. Midge, get a clean cloth. I don't want to eat on a table covered with a lot of dirty money."

"Dirty?" Charlie chuckled. "You mean dirty because Joe didn't earn it? Or dirty from too many people's hands?"

"Both," Mom replied promptly. "Get it off and we'll eat. You can count it afterward. I give up."

With a clean tablecloth, Midge and Nora quickly reset the table while Mrs. Drew turned back to dishing up the stew. She knew when she was licked.

When supper was over and Joe and Charlie and Pop counted the coins, they found Joe had earned $36.40. Charlie and Pop looked at each other.

Pop just shook his head. "You know, of course, usually money not earned isn't 'good' money. I've never taken a dishonest dollar in my life. But it would be impossible to return all this. Maybe the Lord meant us to have it. Most of this can be saved for your school needs."

Satisfied with that solution, he helped the boys scoop up the money and put it into jars for safekeeping.

Later Pop checked with other paper boys and found they all had done almost as well in tips alone. The end of the war was worth much more than the beginning, as far as newspaper boys were concerned.

After the false alarm on November 10, 1918, the real end of the war on November 11 was an anticlimax. Climax or anticlimax, that was a lot of money for a nine-year-old boy to have at one time.

Four

Sister Elsie Dies

CHARLIE WAS A FAMILY BOY. He enjoyed being with his family, and he enjoyed doing things for them. For this reason he became aware, almost as soon as his mother, that things were not quite right with Elsie.

Elsie, a slim, very fair girl with light brown hair, seemed to become more quiet each day. She had begun to cough a great deal, but no one paid much attention.

Influenza had been sweeping the country for months. Although many people were ill, it apparently had not affected the Drew family. True, Elsie had not felt well enough to attend graduation exercises for Charlie and Midge that spring, but she often felt tired. The family had not thought much about it.

The summer of 1918 was unusually hot and muggy, with high humidity and temperatures in the nineties most of the time. Elsie, lying in bed and often wringing wet with perspiration, had to be sponged off frequently. She did not complain, but lay quietly, her hazel eyes so much like her father's, watching the activity around her. The doctor did all he could to make her comfortable, but no medicine seemed to help.

After Charlie and Midge entered Dunbar High that fall, Mom could not keep her worries to herself. She could not understand why Elsie should be so frail. She and Pop even wondered if moving to a different climate might help, but they loved the old home and their roots were deep there.

Flu was now hitting every part of the nation and people were dying at an alarming rate. With the exception of Elsie, the Drew family stayed well. And in spite of the flu, Elsie more or less held her own during that winter. But in the spring of 1919, she died quietly one night in her sleep. It was a terrible shock to the entire family.

Charlie, now fifteen, could not bear the thought of attending school for a few days. Elsie's death sobered him as nothing else ever had. After all, she had been only two years younger than he. His always-active hands, most expressive when he was excited or interested in something, were quiet. Could a different doctor have saved Elsie? Why had she been ill so long?

He began to wonder what being a doctor would be like. Would it be possible to find answers for deaths similar to Elsie's? Maybe—just maybe—he could study medicine sometime. It was such a new thought that he dismissed it almost as soon as it entered his mind. No one in the family had ever been a doctor.

Mrs. Drew blamed herself for letting the family continue to live where the swampy land bred mosquitoes. Foggy Bottom was indeed well named. Since she herself did not always feel too well, with bouts of chills and fever, the doctor began to suspect malaria, although he never diagnosed it as such. Even Mr. Drew at last thought a change was advisable.

Actually, it was Elsie's death that decided the family. The house had lost its happy air. Nothing there could ever be the same. So they would move. The long hunt for a new home began, and at last they found a spot in Arlington they felt had possibilities. There would be no quick change, however. It still needed some thinking through.

Meantime, the United States Government was buying up property in the Foggy Bottom area. Already enough construction was going up near them that Pop often took the children to watch. He predicted that some day most of the area would be covered with government buildings.

Then the Department of the Interior decided to erect a building near their park. The children always thought of Rawlins Park as "their" park because they played there so much. They loved the great pink-blossomed magnolias and the horse-chestnut trees. It would not be easy to leave all this, but it *was* an excellent time to make a change.

It was not easy for the family to settle down to actually making the move. So many things had to be considered—especially the children's schooling. If they moved to Arlington, just across the river in Virginia, would it still be close enough for Charlie to attend Dunbar? This was important, but he felt that as long as his trusty bicycle held out, he would be able to go anywhere, and there were always the trolleys.

Charlie also felt that the sooner they moved, the better. In spirit, Elsie still seemed to be in the house, and he knew that Mom, especially, grieved. To be sure, they all did but tried not to show it.

At last Charlie and Midge's first year at Dunbar High was over. Charlie, now almost six feet tall and sturdy, did exceptionally well in sports—basketball, football, track, and baseball. He had put swimming into second place and never again would enter competition. Joe became the swimmer of the family; he was a faster swimmer and a better diver than his brother.

Nora, now six, and a replica of Charlie, was an active little girl. Although she was never as sports-minded as her brothers, she managed to hold her own with the older children in other ways. Her hair was a soft brown rather than black, but she had her mother's fair coloring. She was always busy "helping" Mama in the kitchen or around the house.

During the summer of 1919, Charlie worked as a messenger at the Y.M.C.A., and this helped financially during his sophomore year at Dunbar. Nora entered first grade while the family was still in the District of Columbia, and Joe was now in the fifth grade. Mom and Pop wanted to be sure of real advantages in any new home they chose, so one more school year was spent in the old home at 18th and E Streets.

As that school year advanced, more and more thought was given to the pending move. Sorting and discarding and packing began in earnest that winter, so there should be no need for last-minute rushing. At last each member of the family began to look forward to the move, to getting away from all the sad reminders of Elsie's death.

Charlie came upon his mother one day, surrounded by great piles of odds and ends to be sorted through, crying over a small rag doll that once had belonged to Elsie. She was holding the tiny doll against her cheek, now wet with tears.

Tears came to his own eyes as he put his arm around her slender shoulders.

"Mom, don't," he begged softly. "Don't cry. Elsie's in heaven. She's all right. Please don't cry." He felt helpless. Gently, he took the small doll from her hand.

"I know she's all right," sobbed his mother, holding both hands over her eyes. Then she grabbed up the bottom edge of her black-and-white-checked apron and covered her face. "But I'm not." Her voice was muffled. "Sometimes I think I can't stand it."

She leaned against Charlie's shoulder and was quiet for a moment, dabbing at each eye with the apron. Finally her sobbing stopped and she took a big shaking breath.

Lifting her head, she said, "Help me up, son. I'm all right now. I'll just be glad when this move is finished."

She never again referred to the incident.

Mom was herself again, but Charlie wasn't. He took the small doll and packed it among his own things. He remembered the time he had helped Elsie make it from one of his old shirts. She had made the little blue dress from one of her own discarded dresses. It was a part of their childhood, now finished.

Sometimes he wondered if God heard his prayers.

Five

Charlie Learns to Study

DURING THE SUMMER OF 1920 the Drew family completed their move into the country. They had found a beautiful spot in Arlington, just across the Potomac River.

The white house stood among maple trees, with apple, cherry, pear, and plum trees nearby. A colorful red-blossomed crape myrtle bush or two were thrown in for good measure. Not native to the area, these were brought in from the South.

The neighbors threw a big party for the Drews before they left Washington, to show they were sorry to lose such fine neighbors and friends.

It made Mr. and Mrs. Drew happy to know they had been so successful as neighbors. Charlie, however, felt their relief as they settled into their new home. Here would be no reminder of Elsie.

Most of their new property had been planted in vegetables. This was fine, if one wanted to earn one's living selling vegetables, but Mr. Drew felt he could not be both farmer and carpet installer.

He was the only Negro member of the AFL. He had been secretary-treasurer for many years, and he could not now jeopardize his position by dividing his interests and time.

That summer he and Charlie and Joe replanted much of the huge yard from vegetable garden to lawn and flower beds. Much time and labor was involved in getting the ground ready for the grass and the many bright flowers and shrubs. Both Mr. and Mrs. Drew always stressed that they should never be afraid of hard work. Busy children were good children.

"Use your hands," Pop was always saying. "Good honest work never hurt anyone!"

Because Joe still had the newspaper business and would have farther to go each morning and evening to handle it, they tried to finish as much yard work as possible before school started. The business had been an important experience for Charlie in management, responsibility, and self-confidence, and it would also help Joe. Only now he would need to be up and out earlier than before.

Discrimination continued to be only a minor factor in the lives of the Drew children. Again, in the country, they had their own friends and knew where they could go and where they could not. Had they wanted to live away from the black community, they could have blended into any society. The Drews were proud of their heritage, however, and saw no reason to deny their Negro background. They felt themselves to be just ordinary Americans.

That fall of 1920, Charlie entered his junior year at Dunbar High. Now he would need to get up earlier than ever. He had little time to help around home, but he began to do better and better in sports. He practiced hard in football, then basketball, track, and finally, in the spring, baseball. He gloried in each sport and was outstanding in all.

Opposing teams learned quickly that it would take some real effort if Charlie Drew were playing against them. Negro teams played only against other black teams. A few black players competed on certain college teams, but any real competition in high school was among blacks.

Charlie often wished he could compete in sports without having to study, but the family philosophy would not let him. One Saturday when he was home and working in the yard, he overheard a conversation between Mom and their next-door neighbor, an older man. They were on the other side of the heavy hedge and did not see Charlie.

Mom probably had taken the old gentleman a fresh pie or a tasty bit of stew. She could not help doing things for the neighbors here, just as she had at their old home.

At first Charlie was not paying much attention to the conversation. Then he heard his name.

Mom was saying, "I just can't understand why it takes Charlie so long to learn his lessons. Joe and Nora don't seem to have any trouble, young as they are. Charlie's never been too interested in studying, I'm afraid." She gave a deep sigh. "I do wonder at times if he'll ever finish high school."

Startled, Charlie stopped hoeing and straightened up. Not finish! Of course he'd finish!

Frowning thoughtfully, he looked out over the newly planted yard. Studying itself wasn't so hard, but what was the future in most of the stuff he was learning? Latin or Spanish—what good were they? Math was all right, and so was biology. Maybe next year he would try chemistry. But English grammar—that really floored him.

Now sports! That was something. *There* was a reason for studying. Everything he could read or hear about sports, he remembered. Someday perhaps he could be a coach—if he did not study medicine. Although he had never mentioned this secret desire to anyone, he was beginning to think about it more and more.

He watched a robin tugging at a worm not far from where he had been hoeing. The soil was rich and things would grow well, but now his mind was far away. Becoming a doctor! *That* would be something.

The neighbor's voice was sympathetic. "Don't worry, Mrs. Drew. There's always one slow learner in every family. Your boy'll finish some day. He's a good boy. He's kind. He was helping me over here just the other day. He'll make out."

Charlie moved away so he could not hear any more and began to hoe again, chopping down hard in the flower bed. It made him uncomfortable to know he had overheard a conversation not meant for his ears.

He stopped hoeing again and scratched one ear thoughtfully. Money for college would not be easy to come by. Pop still earned just enough for the family needs, but nothing extra. Studying medicine, or even continuing in the sports world, certainly meant college. Whichever way the wheel turned, it had to be college.

Well, one thing at a time. The hoe hit the weeds hard again. He would get through high school first. Maybe he could even bring up his grades to please Mom.

Charlie did bring up his grades, to the great pleasure of his mother. At the end of his junior year the Drews were delighted to learn that Charlie had won the James E. Walker Memorial for outstanding athletic ability and citizenship. For the first time, he felt that possibly more concentration on his studies had some merit. It did make him feel good to know he had won that coveted award.

Pop was proudest of all that his boy Charlie had done so well. He felt now that his older son would really go places in athletics.

Six

An Athletic Scholarship to Amherst

DURING THE SUMMER OF 1921, Charlie worked in the glass fac-
tory in Salem, New Jersey. It was hard, dirty work, and some
of the fellows did not even stay the entire summer. But Charlie did! He earned good money, but it made him realize he
wanted something more than a laborer's job. When he entered
Dunbar again that fall for his senior year, he began to study
harder.

Until now, he had taken only a half-hearted interest in the
sciences. He found he did not especially care for chemistry and
physics, but he did like biology and math. He knew, however,
that to go on to college he would need more preparatory courses, if possible. Before, his highest grades had been in physical
education.

Pop now began to stress some of the problems of going out
into the world. Charlie soon learned that when Pop mentioned
"going out into the world," he usually meant the white world.

This was done quietly, with no thought of upsetting the
boys or making them antagonistic toward white people. Both
Pop and Mom knew that sooner or later they would have to
face problems they did not face in the Negro community. All
their children would.

"Never run away from problems," insisted Pop. "Face them squarely! You don't solve anything by running away. And stay clean, boys! Stay clean! Colored boys don't have a chance if they get into trouble with white people."

Neither boy ever forgot that excellent advice.

One thing happened that winter which at first made Charlie unhappy. Eva, a new sister, was born on December 12.

Charlie was eighteen. Mom and Pop had no business having more children. It made him feel conspicuous in school. At first he dodged his friends, but soon his natural love of young children and consideration for his mother took over. He was finally able to accept this new development when he saw how pleased his mother was.

"God sent this baby to fill our hearts in place of our dear Elsie." Mom's voice was warm, her eyes happy. Each member of the family seemed to find new peace and pleasure in the arrival of their beautiful Christmas baby.

Eva had golden hair and blue eyes. Eight-year-old Nora could not keep her hands off the baby. Playing with Eva was like playing with a live doll. Nora loved to have the tiny fingers curl around hers, and her hair was as soft as Mama's best dress. Nora's watchful care of the new little sister gave her mother many restful moments.

As Eva became older, Pop played with her after work, often taking her with him if he had errands to do. She learned to swim before she could walk. He said she took to the water so naturally, she was the easiest of all his children to teach.

Charlie did well in sports again that winter. He also did better in his studies. He sometimes wished he had not bothered with chemistry; he liked biology much better. He liked to explore the bodies of animals and insects, learn about bones and nerves and muscles. What would it be like to study the human body?

As the school year advanced, Charlie thought more and more about college. He knew now he did want to go. It would no doubt be Howard University, since Howard was close by. And it was one of the top Negro universities. Also, Mom had graduated from Howard, and it would be nice to attend her alma mater.

Being a four-letter man had its responsibilities. Whether it was basketball, football, track, or baseball, Charlie was outstanding. As a sprinter he could beat everyone. He became captain of a company in the High School Cadet Corps, a form of military training that taught leadership, discipline, respect for authority, and such things.

He also won the James E. Walker Memorial medal again; he was popular with his teachers, as well as with his classmates. Although his athletic ability was so great he could not be denied the honor of receiving the Walker medal a second time, this was the last time one person would win it twice. Thereafter it went only to a senior.

Charlie graduated from Dunbar High School in a blaze of glory. The big item was an athletic scholarship to Amherst College in Massachusetts. Help from home and money he would earn during the summer would supplement the scholarship fund. He was most grateful for the help.

With the approach of fall Charlie began to find it hard to realize he was leaving home. He'd never been away for any length of time. The day finally arrived to say good-bye.

"Young people have to learn to be on their own," said Pop, giving him a firm handshake, then whacking him across the shoulders. "Young birds have to try their wings." He turned away suddenly.

Charlie swallowed a lump in his throat as Mom kissed him and hugged him. She didn't say much and neither did Charlie. Years later he learned she had not wanted him to go so far away. Howard University was good enough for her; it should have been good enough for her children—for Charlie, the eldest, the first to leave the nest.

Seven

A New World to Conquer

ENTERING AMHERST COLLEGE THAT FALL OF 1922 with white schoolmates was like being faced with a new world to conquer. Charlie, however, did not feel set apart from the others after he got used to them. He was simply another student.

More than once he thanked his stars that Mom and Pop had made him study so much. It had been Pop who'd made him see the necessity of hard work and good sportsmanship, no matter what happened.

If any young man was ready to face a white world with its many problems, Charlie Drew was that man. Some things a black man could do, and some he couldn't. It was as simple as that. If discrimination were to rear its ugly head, he would surely find a way to overcome it!

Charlie treated everyone just as he had at Dunbar. A friendly "Hi!" here and a cheerful "Hello!" there quickly brought many new friends. He tried to follow poet Emerson's advice: "The only way to have a friend is to be one."

He was careful in regard to girls. He was a handsome, 195-pound, 6'1", well-built athlete, and it was natural for girls to be attracted to him. He knew this was an especially dangerous area. He had heard older friends at home describe what could happen if a Negro man went out with a Caucasian girl. Neither race liked it. The girls might find it frustrating not to be able to catch his interest, but at least he was not giving them more serious problems.

Actually, the white world did not seem nearly as bad or as frightening as he had been led to believe. This was his feeling in the beginning.

Charlie liked Amherst. He took a liberal-arts curriculum and found the classes challenging and the teachers stimulating. If he did not particularly care for English and other languages, he did find the sciences fascinating. He proved to be adept at further study in biology. He also liked mathematics well enough that, for a time, he considered majoring in engineering. He learned, however, that this was a hard area for a black man to break into.

But sports continued to hold most of his interest. On the first day of practice Charlie was glad to see he was not the only black player. The first year was a proving ground for four other capable young black men. One, Bill Hastie, was a childhood friend.

In football, George Gilmer was the fastest back on the team. Ben Davis was a tackle. In track, Bill Hastie and Monty Cobb were outstanding. As a halfback fast on the getaway and explosive on inside plays, Charlie became the star of the freshman football team that fall. He also led in basketball. It was unusual for a student to become a star so quickly.

Again he excelled in both track and baseball the following spring. In track he was the only member of his class to win a major letter during his freshman year. His sprinting was lightning fast; no one could begin to keep up with him.

In his sophomore year Charlie won more laurels. Having Tuss McLaughry as his football coach gave him a confidence nothing seemed to shake. Coach McLaughry had a way with all his players that seemed to inspire them to do their best. One outstanding play was never forgotten by anyone who saw it.

It was almost the end of the 1923 season. Thousands of fans were cheering and stamping. Gaily uniformed cheering sections made the stands sparkle! Amherst was trailing Wesleyan University, six to ten; it was the last play of the game.

30

Tacklers had been hanging all over halfback Charlie Drew, and the other two black men on the team had been as busy as Charlie. Gilmer had run a kickoff for a touchdown, with tackles Davis and Drew taking out the last man.

Only seconds to go!

Now or never! thought Charlie, and he desperately heaved a tremendous pass across the goal line to John McBride. McBride's leap up into the midst of a sea of frantic Wesleyan arms was spectacular. He snared the ball for a touchdown! It was a forty-yard throw, giving Amherst a precious victory of twelve to ten.

The fans went thundering, shrieking wild! They had never seen anything like it! "Charlie!" they screamed. "Charlie Drew! *Charlie!* CHARLIE!"

Coach McLaughry, remembering years later, said, "Charlie Drew was able to throw the old pigskin farther and with more accuracy than anyone I ever saw. He was an excellent receiver and was equally effective on the defense; a true tackler, a pass-stopper. He had unusually tremendous vitality, able to get a second wind when other players were all through."

This built up such team confidence in Charlie that Amherst, at its peak in 1925, rolled up its largest score in Little Three history (Williams College at Williamstown, Massachusetts; Wesleyan University at Middleton, Connecticut; and Amherst). That year Amherst lost only to Princeton University.

With Drew and Davis on the team, this was the first time Negroes had played against Princeton since 1915, when Paul Robeson had been mauled so badly at Rutgers that he had been hospitalized for almost two weeks. Charlie and Ben were told about this, but they felt they could hold their own. Coach McLaughry talked with Coach Roper of Princeton, and they agreed there would be no foul play.

In spite of this Charlie and Ben soon had a taste of what discrimination and dirty play were like. There was no foul play as such, but Charlie had never before had so many "accidents" in one game. He soon realized he was expending energy just to stay on his feet. With one exception, his speed and marvelous agility carried him through. Then once, without any warning, he was spilled.

A tremendous shout went up from the Princeton side. When he heard those shouted derogatory remarks and names, Charlie realized that here was something he could not fight. He felt his face flush that dark red color that earned him the nickname Big Red.

Furious, he was on his feet in a flash and playing harder than before. He was not seriously hurt but the odds were against him. Amherst lost. Actually, they had not been expected to win because Princeton was *the* team at that time.

In spite of this, Charlie Drew was the real star of the game. He gained more than 160 yards for his team.

Eight

Discrimination Rears Its Ugly Head

IN HIS JUNIOR YEAR, ANOTHER INCIDENT, also having to do with discrimination, stood out in Charlie's memory; this incident was never forgotten by any of the four black men involved. It took place immediately after a track meet at Brown University in Providence, Rhode Island.

The four Negroes on the Amherst team were George Gilmer, who ran the sprints; Bill Hastie, the quarter-mile and half-mile; Monty Cobb, the mile and two-mile; and Charlie Drew, high hurdles, shot put, high jump, and broad jump.

Charlie was not with the team when the Amherst athletes went to Providence. He had gone ahead to Boston so a doctor could check the leg injury received in a football game. The doctor pronounced the leg completely healed, and Charlie was happy to be able to join his teammates.

He arrived at Brown just in time to take the field with the rest of the team. Naturally, there was great rejoicing and much back slapping over his return.

In spite of the injured leg, now healed but still slightly sore, Charlie piled up an impressive score. The meet was close, and although the four black men won a substantial number of points for the Amherst team, Brown University won.

Afterward, when the team showered and changed into street clothes, the four young men were the last to leave the dressing room. The minute they stepped outside, Charlie sensed something wrong.

The rest of the team, standing quietly near the convoy of limousines that had brought the players, looked puzzled and uncomfortable. The head coach, the coach of field events, and the student manager were in a huddle.

The four blacks stood still, staring toward the group.

"What gives?" asked Bill.

"Don't know," said George, "but I don't like it."

The manager was approaching. He looked anything but happy. "Say, fellows—" He swallowed, then tried again. "Would you—"

Charlie looked at him. The guy was really bothered about something. He was a good manager and the team liked him.

Monty spoke up. "All right! Let's have it. What's happened?"

Charlie glanced at him. His voice was unusually sharp.

"Would you mind eating in the Brown commons?" The words came out with a rush.

"The commons!" Charlie exclaimed. "I thought—the Narragansett—"

"Don't think!" George's voice cut in. "Don't you get it?"

The manager swore, the only time Charlie ever heard him. "Fellows, I'm sure sorry about this. I really am! But when the hotel heard we had black boys on the Amherst team, they sent word they couldn't serve you."

"Couldn't? Or wouldn't?" muttered Bill.

"Is the whole team going to eat at the commons?" Charlie asked curiously.

The manager looked uncomfortable. "Well—no—with reservations already at the Narragansett . . . uh. . . . They did say, though, that they'd serve Doc Newport."

As long as he lived, Charlie never forgot the sinking, letdown, horrible feeling. What kind of crazy mixed-up world was this, anyway? The trainer, Doc Newport, was black, and they would feed him! Fleetingly, Charlie wondered if they'd "serve" him in the kitchen.

Two other thoughts flashed through Charlie's mind. Colored boys were good enough to play their hearts out and get bruised up for the glory of good old Amherst, but obviously were not good enough to eat in the world of whites; and the team was letting them down. Hadn't they even considered eating in the commons with them?

This was one of the very few times Charlie let his feelings show in regard to racial inequalities. He was Big Red for a long time.

It was quiet as the four Negro men ate alone in the Brown commons. They were tired and had been hungry, but not now.

Each fellow rode back to Amherst in a different car in the convoy. The silence in every car was painful. Seldom was the episode ever mentioned again, even among the young blacks themselves. It just took the heart out of some of their playing.

At last Charlie had to admit that discrimination showed up in many ways, some subtle and some vicious, and it was not always possible to do anything about it. But because he liked the sports world, he continued to give his best. It was simply his nature.

In each of his first two years, Charlie won the Cobb Pentathlon Trophy, which gave him permanent possession. At the end of his junior year, he was awarded the Thomas W. Ashley Memorial Trophy, an emblem for the football team's most valuable player. In 1925 he won All American honorable mention as an All Eastern halfback.

In track, he scored each year in the New England intercollegiate; he won the high hurdles and was fourth in the high jump in his final year. One hint of Charlie Drew's phenomenal speed is the fact that after he turned to track, he won the Junior National A.A.U. high-hurdles championship.

The racial problem came up again when it was time to choose a football captain during Charlie's junior year. It was customary at Amherst for the outstanding third-year man on each team to be elected captain for his senior year.

There was no question that Drew was top man, unchallenged in football and track. Normally he would have expected to be chosen captain of both teams.

There was much campus discussion. Many students were for him; some were against. Two logical candidates for captain in the class ahead of Charlie had been passed over because they were Negroes.

Would Charlie also be passed over? . . . He was!

Too many people, however, did not like this third reversal of custom and began a campaign to change the decision. The conscience of the college was finally aroused amid much open criticism; it became the number-one discussion on campus. And when track election was held the following spring, Charlie was unanimously elected captain.

Charlie weathered the storm in his own calm way. Harsh things might have been said among the black students, but white students never heard them. Never one to "carry a chip on his shoulder," Charlie Drew learned to take in stride the good and the bad, in racial matters as with everything else.

It was a continual wonder to him, however, that when a man's accomplishments were equal or better than those of another, skin color could cause such violent and often vicious attitudes. It was unfair, but he knew now he could do nothing about it. Though he had "Negro blood" in his veins, his actions and accomplishments should speak for themselves.

Charlie Drew's accomplishments while at Amherst were not only in athletics. He wrote the words to the national hymn of the Omega Psi Phi social fraternity to which he belonged. He did not write the music, but only because his college mate, Mercer Cook, later professor at Howard University and still later at Spelman College in Atlanta, Georgia, seemed to have more ability. The song became very popular.

In one examination in chemistry, Charlie received a mark of 100 percent, something that happened so seldom no one could remember the last time. Amherst finals counted one-third of the year's final grade. He had done almost as well in biology, his favorite academic subject. Charlie was beginning to hit an unsuspected intellectual stride.

Upon graduation, Charlie Drew was repaid for all the unpleasantness of the past four years. He was presented with the Howard Hill Mossman Trophy, a magnificent silver cup given to the man each year who had contributed most to Amherst athletics during his entire four years.

This official recognition took much of the sting from some of the bad memories, and having his mother and father present at the ceremonies gave Charlie deep satisfaction. He was

36

amused at "baby" sister Eva, now a long-legged, bright-eyed five-year-old who could hardly contain herself. This was her first long trip away from home, and she found it exciting to see her big brother in his graduation cap and gown.

It was indeed a happy time for all.

Nine

Charlie Becomes Coach at Morgan

AFTER HIS GRADUATION FROM AMHERST, Charlie Drew did exactly what he had planned. He became coach, athletic director, and teacher at Morgan State College in Baltimore, Maryland, the following fall.

In the two years he was there he developed many stars. Under his coaching, the Morgan Bears became a first-class football team and won national honors. He brought both the football and the basketball team into collegiate-championship class.

Mr. Drew, an instructor in biology, was extremely popular with both students and faculty. He was interested in everything and so versatile he would try anything. He continually practiced on a battered second-hand saxophone, which brought him much good-natured razzing about his musical ability. No one could find fault, however, with his fine baritone voice, which could often be heard as he joined in on the old school songs.

In spite of his success Charlie began to feel uncertain that he wanted to continue coaching. It did not seem to give the real satisfaction he had expected.

Once in a while he would think of the injuries he had received in football, some serious. One could not live on awards and trophies. Every ballplayer suffers injuries sooner or later, but what is left after the glory and shouting? Sports are fine as hobbies, or for kids, but did he want to direct sports all his life? He did a lot of thinking.

One injury had left a fine hair-line scar on his right wrist. A small infected bone had been removed shortly before he came to Morgan. It had been exceedingly painful and many times he had wondered if he could ever again use that hand freely, but continued exercise and use were bringing it back to normal.

The wrist was still sensitive and as he rubbed it he thought of the time he had been in the hospital. When he closed his eyes, he could still see the bright, clean operating room, the brisk sterile-robed doctors and nurses. He had a good foundation in science. There was no real reason for him not to try the field of medicine.

As Mr. Drew entered his second year at Morgan State with apparent interest and enthusiasm, he was still uncertain. He continued to give his best that entire year, and his colleagues and students never dreamed he was thinking about a change. His father took a craftsman's pride in his work, and Charlie had inherited that passion for excellence, so he was able to carry on as usual.

Toward the end of the year he applied for entry into the medical school at Howard University. He would have to give it a try!

He was at home with Joe when he received the reply from Howard. Eagerly he opened the letter, read it, then read it again. It could not be right!

"Something the matter?" Joe inquired. "Bad news?"

"Well, I'll be—!" began Charlie. He looked up. "They've turned me down! Howard—has—turned—me—down—for—medicine! They want me to coach." He was not used to being turned down—not by his own people. And by Howard, of all places!

"Amherst is one of the best colleges." Joe looked puzzled. "Aren't your credits any good?"

Charlie began to gesture. Then he hit the table with his fist. "Not a thing wrong—except I don't have enough! In *English!* Short two. Need eight!" He could not keep the disgust from his voice. "Six credits are good enough for other colleges, but not for Howard! How do you like *that?*" He was completely overcome at the audacity of the refusal.

"They don't even give me a chance to make them up." His voice was bitter. "I'm going to run that place some day! Just—you—wait!" The table jumped each time his fist hit. "And not as a coach either!"

Indeed, Charlie Drew had been offered the post of assistant football coach at Howard. They knew about his success at Morgan. But he had had two years of coaching, and it was not what he wanted. Why should he continue in that field at Howard?

In his reply, he thanked them, but added, "If my English isn't good enough to become a medical student, I'm sure it would never be good enough for a faculty post in the department of physical education."

His mother was most unhappy. She could not understand why Howard University was not willing to accept her son in any capacity he wanted.

Charlie had saved enough money while at Morgan to continue at least for a time in further study—if he could find a place to study. Now he was more determined than ever to study medicine, and since Howard had turned him down, he began to think of other colleges. Not all were accepting Negroes, as he well knew, and some medical schools were definitely better than others.

Ten

A Desire to Study Medicine

In 1928, Joe, who entered Dunbar High School in 1923, had
just finished his first year at Howard. In his senior year at
Dunbar, he too had won the Walker Memorial. He was planning to become a physical education instructor and probably
would teach in the Washington, D.C., schools.

Charlie was happy that Joe was doing so well. When Joe
told him about the new Francis Swimming Pool opening that
summer, the two young men decided to apply to become life-
guards. They got the jobs—Charlie as manager and Joe as
head guard. During other summers, Joe became manager.

Another guard of note was Frederick Douglass, great-
grandson of the late greatly revered abolitionist. Fred and the
Drew boys became good friends.

Although Charlie was still an excellent swimmer, his interest had turned to other sports. Joe, on the other hand, had
perfected his swimming and also his diving, and Charlie was
hard pressed to keep up with him. The brothers had been fairly evenly matched, but Joe, because of continual practice, was
now the stronger swimmer.

They took training in lifesaving and first aid through the
American Red Cross, and would teach anyone, young or old,
who wanted to learn to swim. The brothers turned out some

fine junior and senior lifesavers who were proud to wear the FSP (Francis Swimming Pool) lifesaving emblems.

Charlie was surprised and delighted to discover that his little sister Eva, now seven, not only was becoming a little beauty, but also was one of the best swimmers for her age in the district. When he took time to teach her new tricks in the water he became her idol, and when he trained the team for meets, he became her coach.

Mr. and Mrs. Drew were still strong forces in the lives of their children. Both parents, and Nora, who usually only watched, would be at the pool for a swim meet, and Mr. Drew helped rub down the competing swimmers. Little Eva would wrinkle her nose at the smell of wintergreen.

Afterward, the odor always reminded Charlie of those delightful summer days when they were all together, enjoying their work at Francis Swimming Pool.

Some of their hardest work occurred when it was time for an AAU meet. It was necessary to follow strict sanitation rules, and everyone got in the pool to scrub it down.

Sometimes the teams would be taken to New York and Philadelphia to compete. Charlie insisted that team members train faithfully and go to bed early. The swimmers did not always want to follow these rules but they found it paid off when they did. Black teams, however, found it hard to achieve any status. Although they might be superior to white swimmers, color was still playing a big part.

As 1928 passed into 1929, Charlie became more and more determined to further his education in medicine. He saved all he could toward this goal, adding a few dollars from time to time by umpiring basketball games. He never passed up a chance to earn an honest dollar, and his father always backed him. Charlie knew Pop would help financially as much as he could; also, student loans were available.

Charlie Drew applied at a number of colleges, and finally picked one whose requirements were not quite so strict. McGill University in Montreal, Canada, was perfectly willing to accept him with his six credits in English.

This university had been outstanding in medical training since the first teaching group, the Montreal Medical Institution, was formed in 1824. In 1829 it had become part of McGill University and was now a well-established medical school.

McGill was noted also for its kindly treatment of Negro students. Charlie had long realized that preparedness in a specific field of professional endeavor meant everything to Negroes. He had learned the limitations imposed by discrimination. Very well, then, he would prepare himself to become so well qualified, he could fit in anywhere.

He began to feel that surgery might be his field. He knew that preparation for this meant a long hard pull. Any money for expenses would have to be made during the summers. There simply would not be time to work during the school year.

But if he could manage it, he would like to turn out again for sports. It was good exercise and also a release from the tension of study.

Eleven

McGill University: 1929

CHARLIE DREW ENTERED McGILL UNIVERSITY in the fall of 1929. His choice was a happy one. Dr. John Beattie, head of the anatomy department, took a special interest in the young man from the States who showed such zeal and talent.

Mr. Drew was precise and thorough in everything he did. He always had a place for everything and everything was in its place, a most important trait for anyone planning research.

He liked the laboratories, with their neat and precise rows of test tubes, ready for experiments. He especially liked the studies and experiments that involved muscles, bones, and nerves in the human body. He wanted to learn everything he could about the body and how it worked.

Dr. Beattie was an excellent instructor and the two men, as teacher and student, worked well together. Their respect for each other personally and professionally deepened with time.

Charlie Drew may have been a dreamer and a thinker, but he was also a man of physical action. He now considered athletic activity as play and relaxation; and he showed he could play as well as he could study.

Although he had been out of competitive sports for two years, the rest apparently did him no harm. He won medals in hurdles, high jump, and broad jump; in one Canadian intercollegiate competition he earned sixty-six points, an all-time record. At the end of his sophomore year he was elected captain of the McGill track team.

But he never once lost sight of his goal to become a surgeon. His one desire now was to make people well and whole.

In his studies at McGill, Charlie Drew soon discovered the importance of blood and blood transfusions in preventing shock after operations. At that time very little was known about post-operative shock or what caused it.

Although Dr. Beattie himself had been studying along these lines, little was then known about blood derivatives such as plasma and serum, and how effective they could be in combating shock. It was thought that whole blood was better.

In World War I it had been noted that shock played an important part in the death of soldiers during the first twelve hours after injury. Refrigerated whole blood was used for transfusions, but this had not been successful because of the difficulty of transporting whole blood and giving transfusions on the battlefield. Almost half the patients died.

Experiments with plasma and serum were being carried out, since both were easier and quicker to give in an emergency. Blood types did not need to be matched as with whole blood. Two cases of interest to Mr. Drew came in soon after he entered McGill University.

The first was a case of shock due to severe loss of blood after a bad accident. Because the patient was obviously dying and there was no time to match blood samples, plasma was given until whole blood could be made available. The patient made such a quick and remarkable recovery that, although whole blood was given as soon as possible, both Dr. Beattie and Mr. Drew wondered if it were actually needed.

The second case was entirely different because there was no loss of blood. Two men badly burned by electricity were brought in. Both were in such a state of deep shock, with rapid pulse and pallid, moist skin, there was little hope for recovery. Quick action again was necessary, and again plasma was used. This brought up the men's vital fluid balance so quickly that the doctors marveled. Both men recovered and left the hospital apparently none the worse for the experience.

Mr. Drew now suspected there was a strong correlation between loss of body fluid—regardless of how it was lost—and shock. Later, while he was interning at Montreal General Hospital, victims of a fire were brought into the emergency room. Again he noticed that shock was more of a problem than the actual burns. Now he knew he had to learn more about this phase of surgery. How important would control of shock be in saving lives? How could body fluid be controlled?

Charlie Drew began to read everything he could find, both from medical libraries and from archives, about blood and its derivatives. The more he studied, the more he felt he had stumbled onto something of real importance.

His research took him back some three hundred years, where the history of blood transfusion was rooted in mythology. It was once thought that, through witchcraft, a young man's blood could restore an old man to youth.

The first successful transfusions from animal to animal were done in Oxford, England, in 1665. Then came transfusion from animal to man in Paris, in 1667. The first transfusion of lamb's blood to a man was successful, but later patients died. A law was then passed prohibiting such experiments on human beings in France.

In London, England, the first successful transfusions from man to man were performed in 1824. Too many individuals, however, died unexpectedly; no one knew why.

In the latter 1800s and early 1900s, doctors began to be aware that certain blood groups did not mix successfully. Much study was needed to find out why some transfusions were successful and some were not.

Mr. Drew went into his third year at McGill feeling as though he were just beginning to accomplish something of real importance. As he worked on his master's degree he gained a new outlook, and he was beginning to do excellent work in surgery.

He also knew there was a depression, and times were hard. News from home was not good. The money he had saved was almost gone, but by being frugal—missing a meal now and then, and not buying new clothes when he could make the old do—he would be able to finish his third year.

He was glad that summer to have the job at Francis Swimming Pool. The depression years were hard on whites, but doubly hard on blacks. Charlie Drew knew about the last-hired, first-fired policy, but it had never applied to him.

He had to have more money. He was too close to reaching his goal to give up or put off finishing his fourth year at McGill. Once he started his internship, he knew he would not be able to continue working summers. He felt an urgent need to seek help, but was not sure just where. He had a few bitter thoughts about the unfairness of life; then he realized he was fortunate to have come as far as he had.

He talked it over at home and finally, realizing this was a real emergency, he wrote to McGill for suggestions about scholarships. He felt his work in the three years he had been there would warrant aid of this kind.

McGill not only could, but did give suggestions. A Mr. Rosenwald, having made a fortune in Sears, Roebuck & Company, was just setting up the Julius Rosenwald Fund of $22 million to be used in scholarships within a single generation. That fellowships be awarded particularly to minorities was one of the stipulations, and talented Negroes were given special consideration.

Charlie Drew's record showed not only that he was one of the most talented, but that he was a hard worker who made that talent pay. Above all, he needed financial help. He was given a Rosenwald Fellowship of one thousand dollars.

When he opened the letter and read, "I have the honor to inform you that you have been awarded a fellowship . . ." it was as though a heavy weight had been lifted from his shoulders. He could breathe easily, and the world looked bright again. He vowed he would repay as quickly as possible, but the only repayment required was that he better humankind in some way.

He graduated second in a class of 137, having been elected a member of Alpha Omega Alpha honor medical society, of which he became vice-president.

Then he won the annual five-hundred-dollar J. Francis Williams Fellowship in Medicine as a result of a rigid examination given to the top five graduating medical students, one of the highest honors open to such students.

The old gentleman next door had been right. Charlie was "finishing some day"; and he was finishing in top form. The slow learner of the Drew family had come into his own!

Charlie Drew's mind wandered back to the time he had first thought about studying medicine. He tried to remember exactly what he had written back in 1928 when he had applied to McGill University:

> My first real urgent desire to study medicine came when my sister died from an attack of influenza in the great epidemic during the war [World War I]. No one seemed to be able to stop it and people died by the hundreds every week. I began to study the sciences diligently.

Perhaps doctors would now have a better chance to keep such people as his sister alive.

At last Charlie's dream was a reality. He had received the degree of Master of Surgery, as well as Doctor of Medicine. He was a doctor and a surgeon, Dr. Charles Richard Drew. He liked the sound of his new title.

Twelve

Charlie's Father Dies

IT WAS 1935, AND CHARLIE DREW, NOW THIRTY-ONE, understandably had thought of marriage now and then. With his present goals, however, he was not ready for that important step. Through the very nature of his contacts, he met more Caucasians than women of color. When he married, he wanted someone with his own heritage. He had never felt any need to "pass." That would mean denying his own family, and he had no intention of doing that.

Two years earlier, Joe, doing well as a physical education teacher, had married Grace Ridgeley, daughter of Dr. Albert Ridgeley, professor of anatomy at Howard. Grace, a graduate of Smith College, was liked by all the family. If Charlie envied his brother his present happiness, no one knew it.

The two years following graduation from McGill were spent as intern (or externe, as it was called in Montreal) and resident in medicine, respectively, in Montreal Royal Victoria Hospital and Montreal General Hospital. Dr. Drew held a rotating internship at Montreal General and served a year as resident in medicine.

Dr. Charles Richard Drew was off to a brilliant career. With the exception of the deep South in his own United States of America, he could now practice almost anywhere he chose. The South was not yet ready for such a "drastic" step.

Then one of those things that can change the best-laid plans happened. Charlie's father became ill and the family sent for him.

Dr. Drew had just arrived at the hospital when he received the wire asking him to come home. He reread the message several times. Pop had pneumonia and was asking to see him. Dr. Drew dropped everything and rushed back to his room. Pop, who had been his mainstay, his pillar of encouragement, needed him.

Charlie caught the next train out of Montreal for New York. There he stopped long enough to pick up a new antibiotic supposed to be effective in combating diseases of the lung. His trip, however, was in vain. Within an hour of his arrival home, his father was dead. That he had become a doctor had not helped, and his frustration at this death was even greater than it had been at that of his sister Elsie.

Charlie's only satisfaction from that particular trip came from seeing the happiness on his father's face at his arrival. At least Pop had died happy that his eldest child was at his bedside.

After the funeral, one of the largest Arlington had seen because many District of Columbia friends were also in attendance, life was never the same for Charlie. There was enough insurance for funeral expenses; the elder Mr. Drew's main insurance, as he was so fond of saying, was in his children.

Joe and Grace, who had been making their home with the Drews, would continue to live with their mother and bear part of the expenses. Joe did not say much. Charlie sometimes felt that his brother too would like to get away. But family ties can be strong and binding, so Joe stayed.

Nora, a graduate of Miners College, had begun teaching the previous year, and she too would help with expenses, though everyone knew her help would not continue. She was engaged to Francis Gregory, a young man studying engineering at M.I.T. (Massachusetts Institute of Technology). They planned to be married and start their own home as soon as he graduated.

Eva was now a slim, pretty girl, just entering her teens. She had adored her father because he had urged her on in swimming and so many things she enjoyed. She would miss him terribly.

Mrs. Drew felt that Charlie should be home. He, as the oldest, should now carry his share of the burden; so Dr. Drew began to do some deep thinking. Did he want to return to Canada, where he knew he could have an excellent career? Or would it be better to try to get on the faculty at Howard University, in order to be close to the family?

He did not hesitate. He applied for an appointment on the Howard Medical School staff. He felt he now had something worthwhile to offer the university.

And Dean Numa P. G. Adams also felt Charlie Drew had something to offer. He appointed Dr. Drew an instructor in pathology. Part of the work would be in Freedmen's Hospital, and this meant Charlie could be home with his mother and the family, carrying his share of expenses. Joe had been helping him financially. Now it was his turn to help Joe continue his work on his master's degree. The entire family rejoiced at the appointment.

Dr. Charles Richard Drew had unusual ability to organize and administer, as had his predecessor, Dr. Daniel Hale Williams, surgeon-in-chief at Freedmen's from 1884 until 1898. Dr. Williams, founder of Provident Hospital in Chicago, had been an excellent teacher at Freedmen's. He had performed the first successful open-heart surgery there in 1893. Dr. Drew also had the talent to inspire and instruct and, like Dr. Williams, would be able to develop his special gift in the area of surgery.

If Dr. Drew found Freedmen's Hospital, in spite of its interesting history, to have rather antiquated facilities, not up to what he was accustomed to, he tried not to comment. He soon realized that the personnel already in charge would not welcome too many changes, so he tried not to press for large or sudden upheavals. Any appropriations came through Congress, and money for many things the staff wanted or needed was not always available.

Freedmen's, originally known as Freedmen's Hospital and Asylum, was the outgrowth of the Freedmen's Bureau, established March 3, 1865, by an act of Congress titled "An Act to Establish a Bureau for Relief of Freed Men and Refugees."

Major General Oliver Otis Howard was selected by President Andrew Johnson as commissioner of the Freedmen's Bureau on May 3, 1865. His principal responsibility was the welfare of the hordes of newly freed slaves that had congregated under appalling conditions in large cities.

General Howard outlined these objectives: "To relieve all the calamities of their situation; to smooth the passage from slavery to freedom; to soothe asperities of the situation and compose the differences that could not be existent after the Civil War; to relieve suffering but in no such way as to lead to pauperism or to interfere with self-support."

Of the ten headquarters established throughout the South, only Freedmen's Hospital was continued after January 1, 1869.

General Howard was also the founder of Howard University. At first the institution was nothing more than an elementary school and social center. Reading, writing, and religious instruction were introduced. Its first diplomas were given to four white girls, daughters of its all-white faculty. By 1901, at the time Dr. Drew's mother graduated, it was fast becoming an excellent institution of higher learning.

Howard University and Freedmen's Hospital continued to develop together. In 1926 Dr. Mordecai W. Johnson became the university's first Negro president; he was still in charge when Dr. Charles Drew became a member of the faculty.

Dr. Charles R. Burbridge, who followed many able men, became superintendent of Freedmen's Hospital during the last years of Dr. Drew's work. In 1936 Dr. Drew became assistant in surgery on the medical faculty of Howard University and surgical resident in Freedmen's Hospital.

Dr. Drew knew that many new facilities were needed. He also knew that the tradition of excellence must be carried on with the limited provisions that were available. One helpful note was that receipts from patients were increasing each year.

He faced the future with great hope. Sometimes he would think fleetingly of the promise he had made that he would some day "run the place." He was not sure whether he was on the way to doing that, but he did indeed face the future with many plans.

Thirteen

A Rockefeller Foundation Fellowship

No matter how he felt about the inequality of opportunity for Negroes and their place in the scheme of life, Dr. Drew had the happy faculty of making people, both black and white, feel comfortable and happy. He had managed very well at Amherst and McGill, and now, for the most part, he was managing very well at Freedmen's and Howard.

His big adjustment was at home. Having taken his place as head of the family, he planned to see that matters continued as he felt his father would want. He made one minor change: Instead of one person giving family devotions, the members now took turns, reading the Bible on Sunday mornings and saying grace at mealtimes.

At first he was not too comfortable about becoming head of the family. Joe had been helping with expenses for so long, it seemed no more than right that he continue in that role. Grace was a good wife and the whole family liked her. To Mom, the five years' difference in her boys' ages made it seem no more than right that Charlie should assume this responsibility.

Charlie was grateful for the happy family relationship. He could see the happiness in his mother's face, and he had to admit he enjoyed the care she lavished on him and the well-prepared regular meals. If at times he felt frustrated over not being able to continue his research, no one knew it. All their money was needed for family expenses.

He particularly wanted to see that Eva had a good education as Pop had planned. She had a talent for painting. It would be nice to have an artist in the family. Perhaps he could even send her to Europe to study.

All her life, Eva would remember how her older brother often gathered the family around him and spent hours reading plays. Members of the family would play the characters, giving their own interpretation to the parts.

Charlie's expressive hands, used to perfection here as he explained how *he* thought a character would act, literally created a world that carried the entire family into the past. If young Eva's rapt attention meant anything, Charlie could be sure he was successful in his attempts.

His favorite book of plays, a thick, red-covered volume, *A Treasury of the Theatre: An Anthology of Great Plays from Aeschylus to Eugene O'Neill,* seemed to dominate the family. No one minded in the least that Charlie was always the director, the rest of the family merely actors, or even just the audience.

Charlie undoubtedly inherited his mother's ability to speak well. Mom might give him suggestions, which he sometimes followed but often did not. In the end he would give his own interpretation, his hands expressing as much as his voice.

Although Mrs. Drew had taken courses in elocution and was a good speaker herself, she felt that each of her children had his or her rightful place in society, and they should conduct themselves accordingly. She gloried in a son who could do many things so well. But Mom gloried in all her children. They were her life.

Charlie remembered overhearing a neighbor woman ask Mrs. Drew how her son was getting along. Charlie was home from McGill on a visit, and Joe had just taken his first teaching position. Mom's quick reply, "Which one?" left no doubt about her feelings in the matter.

With all the children grown except Eva, Mrs. Drew began to take a more active interest in civic affairs. She was already deaconess of the Nineteenth Street Baptist Church, but after Mr. Drew's death, she threw herself into community projects with new zeal.

She founded and was president of the Jennie Dean Community Center Association, and she was the driving force behind the Veterans Memorial Y.M.C.A., the first Y.M.C.A. in Arlington, for which nine of the women members of the Community Center gave lots. The club also worked to obtain a playground for Negro children. Charlie was glad Mom was able to find release in this way from her sorrow over Pop's death.

It was during this time that Nora and Francis Gregory were married. The wedding was beautiful, and Charlie was proud of Nora, a trim, brown-haired figure in her white wedding gown, standing beside handsome Francis Gregory. They were very much in love and Charlie knew they would be happy in their new home. How he wished Pop could have been there to give the bride away!

Perhaps Nora had a special place in Charlie's heart. People always said they looked alike—the same-shaped head and the same penetrating expression in their dark eyes.

While Nora was still at home, Charlie was often amused that girls would try to get to him through Nora and Eva. After Nora left, Eva did not take such an interest in getting her big brother married off.

Dr. Charles Drew was indeed an eligible bachelor. His sisters had tried to be helpful, but Charlie, now carrying the responsibilities of the home and in a new and exacting job, could not yet see marriage as a goal. Perhaps he just had not met the girl who would spark the interest that leads to marriage.

At the hospital, he was still trying to carry on his studies of blood, plasma, and serum and their relation to shock. An intense man, he was busy thinking out problems even when in apparent repose. He would never be satisfied until he had all the answers—or at least most of them. If only he had more time for study, more time for research!

Still, he felt he must keep an eye on Eva. She was too pretty for her own good, was not particularly interested in school (but then, he hadn't been, either, at her age), and certainly needed a strong, guiding hand. Mom was too easy with her. Eva had a definite talent in the arts; but as a teenager, she wanted a good time now, not a brilliant name in the dim and distant future. This would be his main goal—to get Eva through school.

By now Charlie's awards and newspaper clippings of achievements and accomplishments were taking up much scattered space. Boxes and envelopes, placed here and there in his office, were filled. He needed time to get them organized. One day he said something about it to Eva.

"Oh, let me fix them!" she exclaimed. "I'll come in each day after school. You get what's needed, and I'll make you the most beautiful scrapbook you ever saw!"

Charlie was glad to have her working on this project. She was where he could keep an eye on her, and it interested her more than her school work seemed to.

A few years passed, and suddenly at thirty-four, Charles R. Drew had a new decision to make. He was offered a General Education Board Fellowship in Surgery through the Rockefeller Foundation.

He had been promoted to instructor in surgery at Howard and assistant surgeon at Freedmen's, he knew his mother wanted him at home, and certainly Eva needed his strong guidance. But in spite of all this, it did not take him long to decide. Here was a chance for more research such as he might never have again. He prayed to make the right decision.

He would take it!

Fourteen

Columbia University: 1938

CHARLIE'S DECISION CAUSED CONSTERNATION IN THE FAMILY. Mom did not see how she could get along without him. Nora, now living happily in her own home, felt he should be in Arlington with the family. Seventeen-year-old Eva was unhappy. She had lost her father; she did not want to lose her older brother too. Only Joe was matter-of-fact.

"We'll manage," he said briefly. After all, they *had* been getting along before. "Grace and I'll see that Mom doesn't need anything. Just remember! It's my turn next."

"I know you will," said Charlie quickly, trying not to notice the disappointment in Joe's eyes. "I'm not forgetting."

The understanding had been that Joe would help Charlie through school, then Charlie would help Joe. Now, with Charlie already looking forward to other worlds to conquer, Joe again would have to wait.

So in 1938, Dr. Charles Richard Drew, with his precious Rockefeller General Education Board Fellowship, entered Columbia University in New York City for further studies in blood and its relation to shock. His previous work with Dr. John Beattie at McGill had whetted his appetite for more knowledge in this field.

In the department of clinical surgery, headed by Dr. Allen O. Whipple, Dr. Drew worked under the immediate direction of Dr. John Scudder, assistant professor of the department. With his knowledge of blood and its relation to postoperative shock, Dr. Drew fit in perfectly with Dr. Scudder's team of doctors engaged in studies relating to fluid balance, blood chemistry, and blood transfusion.

This was a most important field for a Negro surgeon to enter, because black students had very little chance to focus on the new discoveries which contributed so much to modern pre- and postoperative care. These subjects concerned a vital area of modern surgical advance, since all operations produce some shock, although usually not in as great a degree as do accidents or war casualties.

Dr. Drew's special field of research was the study of blood, and blood derivatives, and their preservation. Perhaps he could call his thesis, the written requirement for his doctorate, "Banked Blood."

Personally, Dr. Drew found the study of blood fascinating. He could never understand why people showed such a reaction, sometimes even horror, at the old superstitions. It would be interesting to study where and how all those superstitions started. Probably the strangest fallacy of all was the reference to "Jewish blood," or "colored" or "Negro blood."

Blood was blood, as Dr. Drew very well knew. In spite of the fact that there was no scientific basis for such prejudice, many Americans would be reluctant, or would refuse outright, to accept Dr. Drew's blood in a transfusion because of his Negro heritage. It did not matter that his heritage also included *Caucasian* blood. One drop of *Negro* blood made him Negro in many eyes. It was that one drop to which so many people objected.

In 1901, four main blood types had been discovered by Dr. Karl Landsteiner, a pathologist born in Vienna, Austria, winning for him the Nobel Prize in 1930. One of these blood types—A, B, AB, and O—is present in all blood, regardless of race or national origin.

Type O belongs to a group of people who can become universal donors. Their blood does not clump; therefore it can safely be given to anyone of any blood type.

A process called *agglutination,* meaning clumping, can be dangerous if the red cells of certain types of blood meet. They are incompatible—that is they simply do not mix successfully.

Because early doctors did not know all this, too often their transfusions were not successful. Matching, or typing, of bloods had not yet come into general practice. Doctors knew that sometimes transfusions were successful; often they were not. They did not know the reasons for the successes or the failures.

Undoubtedly the successful ones had received blood from an O donor or a compatible blood type. It was all very complicated, a process that needed much study to discover the whys and wherefores of success or failure. As part of Dr. Drew's work toward his doctorate, he would try to find answers.

Not all was paperwork or research in the laboratory; part of Dr. Drew's work took him into the field. In the North he was able to enter "white" hospitals freely to give talks and demonstrations, but in the segregated South, he was accepted only in Negro hospitals.

In April of 1939 he was on such a trip to speak at Tuskegee Institute in Alabama. This was an oasis in the South for medical information, a tiny clinic where, once a year, doctors from the backwoods came to hear the latest in medical advances and accomplishments.

Dr. Charles Drew was highly regarded by his colleagues. Nurses, as well as physicians, liked to hear him speak; friends who were not even in medicine sometimes came to hear him.

Such a person was Dr. Mercer Cook, an old friend from college days. Dr. Cook was now professor of languages at Spelman College in Atlanta, Georgia, a fine college with fine teachers. Although not a medical doctor, he always liked to hear Charlie speak.

Spelman College for women, originally endowed in 1881 by the Women's American Baptist Home Mission Society, later was endowed by a Rockefeller Memorial in the name of Laura Spelman Rockefeller.

Dr. Drew and Dr. Cook greeted each other affectionately. Then Professor Cook said, "How about coming with me to a party tonight? I know someone I'd like to have you meet."

Dr. Drew just looked at him. "Not you too! Everyone's trying to marry me off! I don't want to get married! Haven't time." He laughed half-heartedly.

Frowning, Professor Cook said sharply, "Look, man, you can't work *all* the time!" He was only half joking. "You, of all people, should know that. Relax! Have some fun once in awhile. Come on with me!"

Dr. Drew sighed. He was tired. "Well—all right." He sounded more resigned than anything. "Since you insist, I'll meet her, but I warn you. . . ."

Professor Cook nodded in satisfaction. "Good! You'll like her. She's from Philadelphia and doing a splendid job as a teacher down at Spelman. See you later." And the two men went their separate ways for the rest of the day.

That meeting changed Dr. Drew's life.

Charlie Drew, eight years old (circled above) with the YMCA boys at the start of the 7-mile hike, 1912.

Photo courtesy of Dr. W. Montague Cobb

Dr. Charles Drew (seated front and Center) in the Rex Club, Dunbar High School, 1922

Charles Drew in Amherst College football uniform.
Courtesy Amherst College Archives

Portrait of Dr. Charles Drew in juxtaposition.

Dr. Charles Richard Drew with wife, Lenore Robbins Drew, and children. (left to right)
Sylvia, Father, Charlene, Bebe, Mother holding Charles, Jr.

General Alfred M. Gruenther (far right), President of American National Red Cross (1957-1964) presenting a portrait of Dr. Charles Drew to members of the Drew family. (left to right) Mr. Joseph Drew, Mrs. Eva Johnson, Mrs. Nora Drew, Miss Bebe Drew and Mrs. Emma (Midge) Sellman.

Fifteen

Lenore Robbins Enters His Life

THE PARTY WAS IN FULL SWING by the time Dr. Cook arrived with his handsome guest.

As they walked through the crowd, Dr. Drew glanced around. It had been a while since he had taken time to relax like this. It was pleasant to see everyone so happy and care-free. He saw a number of people he knew, nodded to some and shook hands with others.

Suddenly he noticed a young woman he had never seen before. How tall and stately she was—what beautiful long black hair and striking dark eyes!

His friend murmured something, then he felt his arm grasped firmly and realized they were walking directly toward her. Dr. Drew could not take his eyes away. Was *this* the person Mercer wanted him to meet?

It was!

As they reached her, he heard Mercer Cook say, "Lenore, have you met Charlie Drew? We went to school together." He turned to Charlie. "This's Lenore Robbins; Minnie Lenore Robbins, to be exact. She's one of our finest teachers."

Gravely Dr. Drew and Miss Robbins looked at each other. How very serious she was.

Then unexpectedly, she smiled. That did it! Charlie could never remember what she wore that evening, but he never forgot that smile.

Charlie Drew, never one to let grass grow under his feet if he wanted something badly enough, lost no time. The sprinter on the track was also a sprinter in life. He had no time for a long-drawn-out courtship. This was the woman he wanted for his wife. On their second date he asked her to marry him, and during the following five months, he did not let her forget it.

Lenore's father worked for the Pennsylvania Railroad. Her mother, a teacher, wrote poetry and had published two novels. Lenore had two brothers—one older and one younger—but no sisters.

On Saturday, September 23, 1939, at four o'clock in the afternoon, Minnie Lenore Robbins and Charles Richard Drew were married in her parents' home in Philadelphia. She was striking in her white dress, with her black hair and sparkling dark eyes. Only members of the immediate families were present.

Charlie, eight years older than his bride, was happy in his choice, but he was as nervous as any bridegroom and was glad when the wedding was over. He was thankful it had been just a small family affair.

They left immediately for New York, where they shared an apartment with another couple. The following Monday morning at eight o'clock Dr. Drew was back at work in the wards at Presbyterian Hospital. They planned to have a real honeymoon later.

Again Charlie had taken his family by surprise, this time by his sudden marriage. Charlie Drew was a busy man and he preferred it this way, with no long engagement. No doubt he felt this marriage was his own and his new wife's business, that he had already given his family much of himself, that it was time to branch out. He was very much in love and had waited a long time for this important step.

He still felt he would see that Joe had his chance to finish his education and that Eva would finish hers. These, however, became secondary priorities, now that he had the responsibility of a family. He was never again to be able to help as he had hoped.

On August 9, 1939, just before he was married, a program had begun which was to have a vital bearing on Dr. Drew's future. Thanks to many able men in the medical world and their investigations of the experimental work sponsored by the Blood Transfusion Betterment Association of New York, the

Experimental Blood Bank of the Presbyterian Hospital in New York was established.

Dr. John Scudder was appointed to direct the laboratory and experimental aspects of the project. Dr. Charles Richard Drew was to manage the blood bank itself and direct clinical investigations.

It was a huge, challenging program and would last only four months, but it dovetailed exactly with Dr. Drew's studies through his Rockefeller grant at Columbia. Not only were his duties numerous and extensive at the blood bank, but he used every spare minute to try to organize his material for his doctoral thesis. He was getting by with very little sleep.

The new Mrs. Drew had not planned to work, but the program was so short and the need so great, both for help at the hospital and money at home, that she took a job in the laboratory. At first she filled in as part-time secretary, but she soon also began to help as technician. About the only time she could be with her husband now was while they were working.

As with all marriages, this one did not always sail smoothly. There was not enough time to relax together, not enough money to always make ends meet, ever-increasing responsibilities. In some ways it was a trying time. Lenore Drew learned early that a doctor's life is not all glamour. But the serious young teacher from Spelman College was able to accept the long hard hours, the lonely hours, the ups and downs—because she too was very much in love.

Mrs. Drew also learned that her beloved husband would give the shirt off his back to help someone or give his last cent to right a wrong. There was one time in particular when this hurt.

In heavy traffic, Charlie had gently bumped the car ahead of them. The woman driver hopped out of her car, ready for battle. Dr. Drew also stepped out, and they inspected the damage. There was only a small dent in the back bumper of the woman's car, so he whipped out his wallet; she was satisfied when he offered her twenty-five dollars.

As they drove on, his wife protested that it was their last twenty-five dollars.

Dr. Drew's only reply was, "We'll manage. God is with us."

Yes, they managed. Young Mrs. Drew learned to manage because she loved her husband, who often was too good for his *own* good.

On June 4, 1940, Dr. Charles Richard Drew finished his research for his doctoral degree. His Doctor of Science in Surgery was the only such degree held by a Negro at that time.

His thesis, *Banked Blood: A Study in Blood Preservation,* submitted in partial fulfillment of the requirements for the degree of Doctor of Medical Science in the Faculty of Medicine, Columbia University, was accepted and placed in the university library for future generations.

This thesis was an imposing document, its bibliography of research and reference materials numbering 417 items. Dr. Drew was thorough and precise. He had checked through books and papers written in French, German, Italian, Spanish, and Russian, as well as English, getting help with translating whenever necessary.

But Dr. Drew himself felt that more study was needed in the area of freezing and drying plasma if it were to be used on a large scale. Experiments had shown that plasma could be more effective than whole blood in some cases. But more research, much more research, had to be done. For the time being, however, his work was completed.

He and his wife and their new daughter, Bebe Roberta, born on August 8, 1940, at Presbyterian Hospital, where both parents had worked, left for their home in Washington, D.C., the city of Dr. Drew's birth. He returned to Howard University to continue where he had left off almost two years before.

Although he had been hoping for a son, Dr. Drew loved his new doll-like, bald-headed daughter, named Bebe (BB, for Blood Bank). He found it pleasant and relaxing to cuddle and play with her. She was such a dainty bit of humanity, with soft, downy skin as fair as his own. But he could not understand why she had no hair.

After settling in their new home at 3324 Sherman Avenue Northwest, Mrs. Drew no longer worked outside the home. She had more than enough to keep her busy there. Later, in 1945, they would make one more move—to 328 College Street Northwest.

It was a happy time indeed for the Charles Drew family.

Sixteen

Blood for Britain

WHILE WAR WAS GOING ON IN EUROPE, and first one country and then another was falling to the enemy, the rumblings were only rumblings in the United States.

Dr. Drew remembered World War I. Then he had been too young; now, for World War II, he was too old. It did not matter; with his new family responsibilities, he should not be thinking about leaving anyway.

If only something could be done to help. Transfusions were slow when blood had to be matched, and it was extremely difficult to give them under the adverse conditions of wartime.

He began to dread picking up a newspaper. As he read each day about the destruction and havoc all over Europe, he unconsciously continued to wonder how he could help.

England as a whole was coming to grips with the unbridled violence of Nazi fascism. In London whole blocks of buildings were being destroyed. Men, women, and children by the hundreds were dying; thousands were left wounded. The British Red Cross was doing all it could to save lives, but help was desperately needed.

What also was needed were ways to freeze or dry large quantities of blood plasma for shipping. Small amounts would not help. Plasma in large quantities was the only answer. There had to be a way!

When Dr. Drew was not operating or teaching, he was in the laboratory working on blood specimens. More and more tests had to be made. Plasma samples had to be tested and retested. He himself was using plasma more and more to prevent postoperative shock.

He thought often of the six miles between Presbyterian Hospital and Mount Sinai Hospital in New York. During experiments, blood had been carried between the two hospitals, and even in that short distance, the agitation, or movement, had caused an increase in plasma potassium. Freshly drawn blood remained clear, while older bloods transported at the same time became cloudy.

Trauma, the separation of agitated blood, caused all kinds of problems, particularly if the blood were a few days old. Shipping whole blood to Europe was certainly out of the question. The time element alone made it impossible.

Plasma was the answer, but should it be shipped in liquid form? Should it be frozen? Should it be dried? Questions— questions—with no answers. Dr. Drew drove himself night and day, hardly taking time to eat, to find answers.

Then one morning in late summer of 1940, a Western Union boy arrived at Freedmen's Hospital. In his hand he carried a cablegram addressed to Dr. Drew.

The white-jacketed doctor, so tired his freckles stood out sharply in his drawn face, took the yellow envelope from the messenger. It would be hard to describe his thoughts as he ripped open the envelope containing the surprising cablegram from Europe.

He glanced at the name of the sender: Beattie. Dr. John Beattie, under whom he'd studied at McGill! What in the world? . . . His tired feeling quickly left him, as he read:

COULD YOU SECURE FIVE THOUSAND AMPULES DRIED PLASMA FOR TRANSFUSION WORK IMMEDIATELY AND FOLLOW THIS BY EQUAL QUANTITY IN THREE TO FOUR WEEKS FULL- STOP CONTENTS EACH AMPULE SHOULD REPRESENT ABOUT ONE PINT WHOLE PLASMA

The doctor reread, frowning deeply. Impossible! Utterly impossible! There wasn't that much blood plasma in the world! Five thousand ampules! Good heavens! He pulled thoughtfully at the lobe of his left ear and took a big breath.

John Beattie was now director of the research laboratories of the Royal College of Surgeons in England. He was in charge of shock treatment and transfusions for the Royal Air Force.

Dr. Drew asked his nurse-secretary to get him a cup of black coffee; then he sat down at his desk to think. His long, sensitive fingers began to toy with first one item and then another. Something would have to be done—but what?

He could not let his old friend down. He, Charles Richard Drew, would not be where he was today if it had not been for John Beattie. John had helped in every way possible when he first began studying medicine. He had shown him everything he knew in the area of blood transfusions and preservation. The two men had done a lot of work together with plasma and serum, and with red and white blood cells. John also knew he had continued his studies in banked blood at Columbia. That could explain the cablegram now on the desk before him.

No, Charlie Drew could *not* let John Beattie down! His eyes glinted and his lips came together in a firm line. He hit the desk with a clenched fist. There just *had* to be a way to lick this problem. What good was knowledge if it could not be used?

First he would send a message to Beattie that there just were not five thousand ampules of dried plasma in existence; but he would see what could be done.

Next, he would get in touch with another friend, Dr. John Scudder, with whom he had worked while at Columbia. In any event, Scudder should know about this request. The entire process of getting large quantities of plasma ready for shipment must be speeded up in some way. That was the crux of the whole matter, and one person alone could not do it.

Dr. Drew had no way of knowing what would happen after his message reached Dr. Scudder. It was possible he might need to return to New York. Perhaps he'd better warn Lenore.

Before Dr. Drew had left New York City for Washington the previous June, he knew that Dr. Scudder had planned to suggest to John F. Bush, president of the Blood Transfusion Betterment Association, then in the process of changing its

71

name to Blood Transfusion Association, that plasma be shipped to France and England. This meant stepping up the volume of plasma produced, which was still a problem. Even the low countries of Belgium, The Netherlands, and Luxembourg were taking such a beating that many people wanted to help in any way they could.

What Dr. Drew did not know was that on June 12, 1940, after he and his family were back in the District of Columbia, John Bush had called a joint meeting of the Association's trustees and the Board of Medical Control to consider this general subject. Dr. Scudder's suggestion was already being seriously considered.

Present at that meeting had been experts in the field, representing the army, navy, National Research Council, Rockefeller Institute, and New York Academy of Medicine. Also present were representatives from the large pharmaceutical companies—Burroughs-Wellcome, Lederle Laboratories, Sharp & Dohme, Parke-Davis, and Squibb.

Dr. Alexis Carrel, the French surgeon and biologist who in 1912 had won the Nobel Prize for his work in blood-vessel surgery and the transplant of organs, had just returned from France. He had pointed out the great need of plasma for war-shocked patients and urged speedy help.

Dr. Carrel and Dr. Karl Landsteiner had been with the Rockefeller Institute for Medical Research at the time Dr. Drew entered Columbia. Both had been members for years until their retirement in 1939.

Dr. Landsteiner also had discovered the Rh factor in human blood and continued to be interested in progress made in all blood research, including plasma and serum. Now he too urged a faster pace in securing plasma in volume.

Dr. Drew greatly admired and respected these men, particularly Dr. Landsteiner, for his splendid work in separation of blood types, which had laid the foundation for Dr. Drew's own work and research.

At the meeting, Dr. Scudder had presented details of the research he and Dr. Drew had so recently carried out through the New York Blood Transfusion Association, part of which dealt with plasma. This had been done in conjunction with certain work simultaneously in progress at the Rockefeller Institute.

Although the use of plasma was still in the experimental stage, it was felt that enough knowledge was available to justify an effort at quantity production. With war casualties mounting, it was time to put to use what knowledge was available for the emergency that then existed.

Immediately following the joint meeting, a special meeting of the board of trustees of the Association had been held. The trustees felt the project should be submitted to the American Red Cross as the dean of humanitarian agencies for war relief.

If the Red Cross were willing, it was voted to sponsor the production and shipment of plasma to the Allies, and to appropriate fifteen thousand dollars from the Association's funds to start the project immediately.

All the technical knowledge and experience the Association had gained in its research would be placed at the disposal of the Red Cross. An immediate preliminary survey of hospitals in New York willing to cooperate in such a program would be made.

Since no data was available concerning the preparation of dried plasma and its efficacy, it was decided that liquid plasma would be used for the time being. It would be bulky, but there was no other alternative. The need was immediate. By the time of the association's meeting with the Red Cross, France had fallen and England was next in Hitler's plans.

Dr. Drew's message reached Dr. John Scudder at exactly the right moment. John Beattie would have help, one way or another.

Things moved fast then. Dr. Drew was called to New York immediately, again with a leave of absence from Howard University.

In September, Mrs. Drew and Bebe would follow. She was not happy about having to pack and move again, but if she wanted to be with her husband, this was what she would do.

Tests began at once for ways to dry and ship large quantities of plasma. No statistics based on casualties in the last war were available to help in estimating requirements for plasma. Everything had to be worked out without benefit of past experience.

A committee, appointed by John Bush, consisted of E. H. L. Corwin, Charles Drew, and John Scudder. They were to make recommendations as to what equipment and personnel might

73

be obtained from the cooperating hospitals and what would need to be supplied by the Blood Transfusion Association.

This Blood Plasma for Great Britain Project, later to be known only as Blood for Britain, was a challenging program. Because it was so terribly needed, Dr. Drew was happy to be a part, to know he was helping the war effort, at last.

Seventeen

Drew Becomes Medical Supervisor

ALTHOUGH THE LIST OF ABLE INDIVIDUALS in charge of the medical and technical side of the blood bank effort was long and impressive, three were outstanding.

Dr. John Scudder, first to propose the shipment of plasma to the Allies in England, helped get the project started. He not only was assistant to the Board of Medical Control but also acted as director of the work at Presbyterian Hospital.

Dr. Charles Richard Drew, as medical supervisor, had charge of coordinating the medical aspects of the program. He was the Association's only paid medical staff member. It was recognized that he had made a great personal sacrifice in giving up his own practice to return to New York for the Blood for Britain project.

A quote from the Blood Transfusion Association files speaks of Dr. Drew's ability to overcome problems, and the respect in which he was held: "Since Drew, a recognized authority on the subject of blood preservation and blood substitutes, and at the same time an excellent organizer, has been in charge, our major obstacles have vanished."

Dr. C. P. Rhoads, medical director of Memorial Hospital and chairman of the Blood Plasma Committee, would also play an important role later in Dr. Drew's work.

Money to launch the program was given by both the Blood Transfusion Association and the American Red Cross. Later each group contributed more, the latter for special purposes, the former for research, bringing the total to fifty thousand dollars.

It is impossible to list the many people who donated their services in the portion of the program for which the Blood Transfusion Association assumed responsibility. Untold corporations, agencies, and individuals contributed to or participated in the work. The New York Academy of Medicine Building, on East 103rd Street, donated space for the project.

Six hospitals—Presbyterian, New York, Memorial, Mount Sinai, Post-Graduate, and Long Island College—became the leading centers for blood donation and preparation of plasma.

Sharp and Dohme was the first laboratory to which the Red Cross sent blood after entering a contract with the United States Army. For a number of years prior to 1941, the company had been making some slight progress in mass production of dried human plasma, but never on a large scale. Also, until now, their blood donors had been paid.

Blood donors, people willing to give their blood without charge, were absolutely vital to the program. While the Blood Transfusion Association in New York was organizing its forces, the American Red Cross in Washington, D.C., was organizing and operating the Blood Donor Service. Both the Association and the Red Cross recognized the problem of obtaining enough blood for their needs.

The combined project actually began operations on August 15, 1940, at Presbyterian Hospital, where Dr. Drew and Dr. Scudder had done so much of their research the previous year.

As a research scientist as well as a surgeon, Dr. Drew felt that much more time was needed to perfect a better method to make plasma safe. While the donor service was being set up, he was using every spare moment of his time still working on this.

Another distasteful problem had arisen. Blood donations at that time were not accepted from Negroes. This was hard for Charles Drew to understand, since he knew, as did many other doctors, how senseless this was. When asked his opinion of the practice, he commented, "My opinion is not important. The fact is that test by race does not stand up in the laboratory."

With the exception of Negroes, blood donors represented every occupation and walk of life. Donors were being recruited by every conceivable method of publicity—over radio, in newspapers, in groups and organizations. Advertisers and the motion-picture industry also responded.

There were about equal numbers of men and women donors; age was limited to between eighteen and sixty. People were not allowed to give blood if their physical condition indicated they might be harmed by it.

The first blood was collected from doctors and nurses themselves at Presbyterian Hospital, followed a day or two later by the Mount Sinai Hospital staff.

The number of volunteer workers was tremendous. These included not only nurses and doctors (both Red Cross and military), but staff assistants, canteen workers, members of the Motor Corps, nurses' aides, and so on. Hundreds of lay and professional workers also volunteered their services and made invaluable contributions in the management, public relations, and recruiting aspects of the service.

Special mention should be given the Red Cross Gray Ladies who acted as receptionists, or hostesses, to greet the donors. They helped quiet the fears of prospective donors, excused delays, gave explanations, and generally looked after their comfort.

Often the care received at the centers determined whether donors would return. Repeat donations were absolutely necessary if the program were to continue. Nurses and doctors learned early that, although at times there might be sound medical reasons for not giving blood, often it was simply a state of mind. Many people even said they felt better afterward.

Dr. Drew thought of the untold man-hours, most from volunteers—doctors, nurses, office personnel, scientists, organizers of all kinds—that had led to the first moment of actual blood procurement for the Blood for Britain project.

The hospitals furnished milk, egg-nog, cookies, or other light refreshments to the donors following the donation. Workers and doctors tried to guard against any sensation of faintness, and donations were always taken while the donor was lying down. A reasonable rest period afterward was suggested—usually ten or fifteen minutes. Although it was thought that aftereffects were only psychological, everything possible was done to protect donors, especially if they felt any faintness.

Now Dr. Drew noticed a donor, a large man, lying on a table, waiting. As medical supervisor of the overall project, he tried to keep in touch with the way things were going. He watched a doctor walk over and swab the inside of the man's arm with iodine and alcohol.

"This may sting for a moment," said the doctor. "You'll feel a tiny prick. I'm going to inject some novocaine so the skin will be numb when I use a larger needle for the blood."

The donor, heavyset and roughly dressed, looked as though he had plenty of blood to spare. This shouldn't bother him. Dr. Drew then noticed the man's wary expression as the doctor picked up the big needle for the actual drawing of the blood. It slipped in so painlessly that the man exclaimed, "Is that *all?*"

"That's all, sir," assured the doctor as he let the nurse take over. "Just keep clenching your fist. That'll speed the process a bit. We don't want you to stay away from your job any longer than necessary." And he went on to the next donor.

Blood was streaming freely into the bottle as the man's muscular hand moved in rhythm with the flowing blood.

Dr. Drew nodded in satisfaction. He liked the nurse's manner. It was matter-of-fact, as though this were simple routine, as indeed it should be. Yet he wanted the donors to know they were doing something important; this also was certainly true.

He knew more donors were waiting outside, besides those now stretched out on the tables. Some were slim girls from offices; some were housewives who wanted to do their share; some were well-dressed executives, too old to go overseas but young enough to qualify for the donor program.

Strict cleanliness and rigid sterilization had cut down considerably on reactions by donors.

As a research scientist as well as a surgeon, Dr. Drew felt that much more time was needed to perfect better methods for making plasma safe. They still were not positive whether plasma was better than serum on a large scale such as this promised to be.

Tests were being made to find a way to dry the huge amounts needed for shipping overseas. Plasma, liquid or dry, was desperately needed *now,* not at some distant date when everything was perfect and all the answers known. Until the drying process was perfected, plasma was being sent to Europe in fluid form, diluted with a saline solution to prevent clotting. This practically doubled the bulk.

All these matters were going through his mind when Dr. Drew heard the nurse say, "We're just about finished, Mr. Smith."

She slipped the tube from the flask to a smaller container fastened to it. Tests would be made from this sample in order to avoid disturbing the contents of the flask.

She applied adhesive tape over the small wound in the man's arm.

"You should lie still a few moments; then you can stop on your way out and get a bite to eat."

Mr. Smith looked at the flask of deep red blood which the nurse was about to place in its rack. Against her orders, he sat up and started to get to his feet. Then slowly, he sat back down.

Dr. Drew casually glanced his way, then quickly stepped to his side as the man lay down again on the table.

"You'll be all right, Mr. Smith," he said quietly. "Just close your eyes and lie still a moment."

The nurse turned from putting the bottle in the rack and reached for some smelling salts. Both doctor and nurse moved quickly without appearing to do so. They didn't want to alarm their donor.

Finally Mr. Smith opened his eyes. He looked rather pale.

"Never fainted in my life," he said. "I feel like a blasted fool."

"Don't feel bad," Dr. Drew told him. "You just sat up too soon. You'll be all right."

"If it'll make you feel any better," said the nurse, smiling, "we've discovered that it's often the huskiest men who become upset at the sight of blood. We had a football player in here not long ago. He fainted dead away when he finished his donation. Giving blood seems to do something to people."

Mr. Smith seemed to be mulling something over in his mind.

"Well, I'll tell you this. I drive a truck, and the girl in our office was bragging the other day about how she's able to give blood without it bothering her. She's done it more than once. If she can do it, by golly, so can I! I'll be in again as soon as my six weeks are up. And that's a promise!"

With that he got to his feet, marched out, and had some refreshments in the outer room. Sure enough, two months later he was in again. He became one of their most faithful donors while the program lasted.

More and more blood was coming in. People all over America were becoming concerned about the desperate plight of people in Europe, especially in London. In the beginning, during June of 1940, one thousand donors had been enrolled to begin the process; within six months, thousands were pouring in. More and more people wanted to donate, and hospitals all over the country were establishing their own blood banks.

With the donor service running smoothly at last, there still were monumental problems to overcome in getting the blood or its derivatives into the hands of the British Red Cross. Tests for drying the plasma were taking time. There were still so many technical difficulties.

Dr. Drew, always ready to meet a challenge, felt this was one of his biggest to date. This was no time to sit back and daydream.

Eighteen

Perfecting Blood Plasma

SENDING THE BLOOD ITSELF TO BRITAIN was impossible because of the time element. Either plasma or serum was the answer, but obtaining either in volume was difficult.

One real drawback, Dr. Drew felt, was that, due to the urgency of the need, mistakes were being made because of lack of information; too few papers had been written on the subject of mass production of either plasma or serum. But papers on new techniques would come later. Now there was time only for personal observation.

During the progress of this work, two schools of thought still continued concerning the best available blood substitute. One side felt that plasma was the answer; the other, serum.

Plasma is the liquid phase of blood, separated from the red cells without clotting; serum is the liquid phase, separated after clotting has taken place. Because clotting often caused serum to be toxic, reactions often followed injections of large quantities.

On December 13, 1940, a number of doctors began a series of experiments to discover whether plasma or serum would be better for such a large project. The Association felt no person was better qualified than Dr. Charles Richard Drew to coordinate this research and pull together the findings of the various groups. Finally, plasma was deemed more satisfactory.

Since this tied in with Dr. Drew's own early research, he was satisfied that plasma was the right product. But no one had yet found a way to separate large quantities of plasma from the red blood cells. And large quantities were vitally needed.

There were no uniform methods for extracting the plasma, although two were being tried—settling and centrifuging, or whirling. Close supervision was difficult because the work was being carried on in so many different locations by so many volunteer doctors and nurses.

Another problem was to find an ideal container in which to ship the plasma. Plastic bottles did not stand up. Metal did not give visibility of contents. Pyrex sometimes broke in transit.

Last, but definitely not least, it was hard to keep the liquid plasma sterile for long periods of time; Britain was also having difficulty. This phase, too, needed more study.

As early as November 1940, the English believed that aid might not be necessary soon after the beginning of the new year. They were beginning to bring up their own volume. Although it was felt that the British need was still great, both the American Red Cross and the Blood Transfusion Association now agreed that no further huge amounts of money should be spent to furnish plasma for Britain. Word went out: Do the best you can with the resources at hand.

Dr. Drew continued his attempts to dry plasma in volume. He knew this would be the only solution to the many problems of plasma delivery. Sharp and Dohme had been doing an excellent job with liquid plasma, but still more was needed, and other laboratories were being urged to contribute.

Finally, information began to come in about one or two stockyard laboratories that used cattle blood by separating the plasma from the red cells in a cream separator centrifuge. As this was being investigated, reports came from England that a modification of such an apparatus was being used there to separate the plasma from human red blood cells.

Dr. Drew and his colleagues became excited. Was this the breakthrough? If this worked, it would take care of securing plasma in volume.

An order was immediately put in for a DeLaval cream separator. The centrifugal force, or fast whirling action, would separate cream from milk. Would it work in the same way to separate the heavy red blood cells from the thinner plasma?

Dr. Drew felt it would. As medical supervisor, he began to completely redesign the separator for the specific purpose of more rapidly, cheaply, and safely obtaining large quantities of plasma. If it worked as the manufacturer claimed, one of the largest problems in mass production of blood substitutes would be solved.

Dr. Drew virtually lived with that separator model until it was as nearly perfect as he could make it. It was tedious and exacting work, and only someone with skilled hands could have done such a superb job.

While he was working on the separator, other doctors had been asked by the Blood Transfusion Association to investigate filters, a very important part of the experiment. Plasma would not filter through certain types, and it was vital that one be found that would eliminate *all* impurities.

The doctors were often frustrated because the need was so terribly pressing. But Dr. Drew could see that everyone was working to capacity. Certain tests just could *not* be hurried. But at last the time came when he felt the drying process could be speeded up; with a larger volume of plasma with which to work, they were nearing their goal.

Neither Dr. Drew nor the Red Cross had wanted to raise too many hopes, but wait until they were sure that orders could be filled, that they could keep enough dried plasma on hand to fill the need. Now the waiting was almost over.

The day finally arrived when Dr. Drew and his fellow workers stood and looked at the great array of bottles in the first step of the drying process. The frozen plasma looked very much like cream on the top of a bottle of milk on a cold winter day. High vacuum action would soon draw the water from the plasma.

Dr. Drew picked up a bottle containing some dry plasma. The pleased expression on his face showed how he felt. Dr. Scudder, standing beside him, smiled. They had reached their goal! The plasma was a flaky, straw-colored substance, with healing properties neither had ever seen or worked with. It could be stored easily, and because it could be put into packages, it could be shipped overseas much more cheaply and safely than in liquid form. Here at last was true success!

Although it was known that plasma could be preserved for months in the liquid or frozen form, the fact that it could be dried and dissolved in water when needed was a step forward.

At any time, at any place in the world, a few moments from now or in years to come, a small amount of these golden plasma flakes could be dissolved in distilled water and injected into the arm of a wounded man, woman, or child. No matching of bloods was necessary, no time lost in finding donors.

It was an accomplishment beyond the wildest dreams of Dr. Drew and his colleagues: At last Dr. Beattie's request could be honored in full!

Nineteen

"Let Him Die!"

ONE EVENING AFTER DR. DREW HAD WORKED LATE, he glanced around the room where so many people had given so much time and effort. He looked at the separator, the vacuum, the many bottles of dried plasma. Much more frozen plasma was ready to go into the vacuum. If only Dr. John Beattie could be here to see what he had started when he sent that cablegram six months ago!

Then Dr. Drew's spirits dropped and he turned away sadly. How long would it be before the American people could take one more very important step? Would they ever be willing to accept the inclusion of so-called "nonwhite" blood in this marvelous process?

As he went out of the big room and down the hall to his office, Dr. Drew thought of a letter he'd shown Lenore only last night, from a woman whose son was fighting in Europe. Although he was her only son, she seemed almost violent in her hatred of the blood bank. She was *not* an admirer of the Blood Transfusion Association program, the Red Cross, or of the wonderful people who were working so hard to save lives.

She had minced no words when she added, "And if my son was dying on the battlefield and only Negro blood was available, I would say, *'Let him die!'*"

Sudden tears smarted in Dr. Drew's tired eyes and a lump came to his throat. Impatiently, he flicked away the moisture from his eyes. This was no time for tears. There was still much to be accomplished. Too many people still felt as that woman did, but this could not slow down the work yet to be done, the lives yet to be saved.

Blood from Negroes had not been accepted at all at first. Now at least it was accepted, but being kept separate. What a senseless procedure, expensive and time-consuming, to continue this segregation of bloods!

In his heart Dr. Drew knew the many places that were not open to him, the many homes he could not enter. Neither could his own blood be used to save the dying sons of such people as the writer of that letter.

And yet—his work and research were helping to save thousands of lives every day. What a touch of irony! The corners of his mouth lifted slightly. Separate but equal! Even to blood that was no different from Caucasian blood. *Would the time ever come?* . . . He shook his head. Surely in God's own time.

Slowly he went into his office and closed the door carefully behind him. He walked to his desk and sat down heavily. Suddenly he dropped his head in his hands—strong, capable hands, which had done so much to help humanity.

He sat very still. Never had he felt so alone.

He raised his head and reached for the telephone. He wanted to hear a loved voice. He wanted to—he pulled his hand back and quickly stood up.

No, he wouldn't talk to Lenore over the phone. He'd go to her instead. She would understand exactly how he felt.

Twenty

A Return to Howard University

DR. DREW SAT CUDDLING HIS BABY DAUGHTER. She was a delightful little girl with such a grave expression as she stared at him with her big dark eyes. She hardly knew her daddy, she saw him so seldom.

He softly stroked the tiny chin, then ran his fingers over the soft dark hair just beginning to come in. Later Bebe's hair would be much lighter, but now it was dark.

Suddenly Dr. Drew sat very still, staring into space. If only he had more time to be with his family, more time. . . .

Bebe decided she liked this stranger after all, and her gurgling laughter broke out joyously. She reached for a button on his shirt, tugged at it with her tiny fingers, and tried to put it in her mouth. Her daddy looked down, held her close, and touched his lips to her forehead. What a joy she was!

Soon his wife came to take the baby for her nap. Dr. Drew put his arm around Lenore and pulled her down beside the baby. Theirs was a good marriage, but they had so little time together. Now perhaps he had a surprise for her.

"Lenore . . ." he stopped, then went on. "Lenore, how'd you like to return to the District of Columbia? Howard University wants me back. I want to go back. Now, if you—"

Lenore kissed him lightly. "Charlie, where you go, I go. I didn't know I was marrying a gadabout. But if Washington is where you want to be, that's where I want to be."

She looked at him gravely as she rubbed her cheek against Bebe's head. "I . . . I thought the Red Cross wanted you to direct their blood plasma program, just in case we get into the war. Didn't you say that England is producing enough for their own use now?"

It was January, 1941. Just a few days earlier, on January 17, the Blood for Britain project had been terminated. A total of 14,556 blood donations had been procured.

"They are," confirmed her husband. "That's the reason I'm trying to make the decision now. What I *want* to do and what I *will* do may not be the same thing. I'm asking you to help me decide."

He held her close. Yes, theirs was a good marriage, but they badly needed more time together.

"What's happening about segregation of blood?" she asked suddenly. "Is that one of the things that's making you hesitate about going on with the Red Cross? It is *so* stupid."

Dr. Drew seemed to be thinking about it. Finally he shook his head slowly. His right hand stroked Bebe's hair.

"Yes, it's stupid and I don't like it! They know I don't like it. It goes against my every instinct to separate the bloods. But I'm honestly trying not to let that influence me in this decision." His grip around her tightened. "I simply want to get back to teaching and practicing surgery. You know that's what I want, what I've been training for ever since I started my medical career."

"I know," Mrs. Drew agreed softly. "This would be a big thing though, wouldn't it? To be the first director of the blood-plasma program for the United States? Exactly what would your title be?"

Abruptly Dr. Drew's hand stopped, held cupped over Bebe's head. "Technical supervisor. Dr. Rhoads has general supervision of the technical operations. I'm technical supervisor. They've asked us to start the program, but I warned them I might not stay." He looked thoughtful. Bebe's small hand was now exploring a pocket.

"You remember Dr. Rhoads was chairman of the Blood Procurement Committee of the National Research Council? He's a good man, a very good doctor. We're to work together to open the first blood center in America for our own armed forces." He sighed. "The Red Cross feels we're qualified because of our experience in the Blood for Britain project. I feel honored, of course."

"But you don't really want it?" His wife looked at him questioningly.

He shook his head. "I don't really want it! There are plenty of good men who can carry on with the program. Earl Taylor is one. If I don't keep the job, he'll go in." Frowning, he continued. "There just aren't many doctors to train young Negro surgeons. I feel I'm needed more in that area, at Howard. They're holding the position open for me."

He stopped for a moment to fondle the baby, who was again trying to put a button into her mouth. How strong she was for her few months!

"It may take a couple of months to get the program started. Then I want to go home. I want more time with you and the baby." He put a finger over the button and little Bebe grabbed the finger.

"Then we'll go back to Washington," said Mrs. Drew happily. "I'd rather have our next baby born there, anyway. Maybe it'll be a boy this time."

Satisfied, Dr. Drew held her tightly and kissed her before she stood up.

"Boy or girl, I love you," he murmured. He kissed the baby lightly on top of her head as Mrs. Drew picked her up.

He sat back watching mother and child disappear into the bedroom. It *would* be nice to have a son. He felt relaxed. It was good to be home on a Sunday afternoon. And it would be good to get back to his practice again. He'd been away long enough. He turned on the small radio nearby. Maybe he could get some symphony music.

While the radio was warming up, he glanced around for his book about Michelangelo. Didn't have much time to read about his favorite sculptor these days—only a few pages now and then. What sensitive hands the artist had had, a sculptor beyond all description. It didn't occur to Dr. Drew that his own hands were very similar to those of the artist he so admired.

89

As music softly filled the room, Dr. Drew opened the book and leaned back again. He was grateful to Lenore for keeping his favorite books within easy reach.

He closed his eyes for a moment, thinking once more of the new blood bank. Yes, he would give them a hand in setting up this plasma program, then he and Lenore and little Bebe would go home—home to stay. He was satisfied he had made the right decision.

The Red Cross Blood Donor Service for the United States armed forces was initiated on February 4,1941. Voluntary donors recruited by the New York chapter gave blood for this purpose in the center organized in the Presbyterian Hospital. During February, 757 donations were shipped to Sharp and Dohme. On March 29, a Red Cross truck, carrying portable refrigerators and other important equipment, made its first trip.

In April of 1941, Dr. and Mrs. Drew and young Bebe returned to Washington, D.C., and Dr. Drew stepped into his permanent teaching post at Howard University.

In that month also, he appeared before the American Board of Surgery for certification as a Diplomate, the top rank in the profession. His was the highest grade of all the candidates who applied.

Although he was now a Diplomate of the American Board of Surgery, Dr. Drew continued to follow the progress of the blood program. He was delighted to learn that by September, ten thousand donors had passed through the center. He continued to feel that the blood-donor center at Presbyterian Hospital was almost a part of him, since he had put in so many long hard hours there, and so very much of himself.

On June 25, 1941, an important step was made in giving Negroes equal opportunity in the working world. President Franklin D. Roosevelt signed Executive Order No. 8802, called FEPC (Fair Employment Practice Committee), prohibiting discrimination in defense industries and establishing fair employment practices. This made Dr. Drew happy, but he did wonder how many would be truly sincere in following this.

In October he became head of the Department of Surgery at Howard University and chief surgeon at Freedmen's Hospital. Much later, he was chosen examiner for the American Board of Surgery. He had indeed come back to "run the place."

For a few months he seemed to lead a dual life—one day immersed in the problems of Howard and Freedmen's; another, following the progress of the blood program in New York.

By the time Pearl Harbor was attacked—December 7, 1941—he knew that all needs could be met in the blood bank. How different it had been during the blitz on London the previous year! He was satisfied, knowing he had had such a large part in it. And he had no regrets that he had returned to Howard University.

His second daughter, Charlene Rosella, born on July 31, 1941, gave him as much pleasure as had Bebe. He was thoroughly enjoying his happy family life and the work he loved. This was where he belonged.

Twenty-One

"Bloods Are No Longer Separated"

DR. DREW'S SURGICAL JUDGMENT AND DIAGNOSTIC SKILL continually amazed his co-workers. One said he liked to watch the doctor's hands because he always seemed to know exactly what he was doing. Another said that every movement was so swift and certain, one knew there would be no wasted time during surgery.

Dr. Drew insisted that manual dexterity was absolutely vital for a surgeon. As a boy, he had always liked working with his hands and playing musical instruments, and now he used his hands for the good of humanity.

But shortly after he returned to Freedmen's Hospital, his diagnostic skill was sorely tried. One case baffled and perplexed him. All indications except one were typical of appendicitis. But that one symptom wasn't at all as it should have been. He took test after test.

One evening the patient, a young woman, was prepared for an appendectomy the next morning. Not entirely satisfied, Dr. Drew kept studying the records. He knew the woman did not want an operation, and he had hoped it might not be necessary.

He went home to prepare for a good night's rest, but continued to think about the case. What *was* wrong? Nothing added up. Perhaps he had better call in another doctor. Having made that decision, he felt better. Still restless, however, he began to check similar cases in his medical books.

When Mrs. Drew asked if he were coming to bed soon, he said he'd be along shortly, but he continued to read.

Finally he found a case that made him wonder. All symptoms except one were the same as those in the present patient. Dr. Drew read further. At last he closed the book thoughtfully and stood up. He felt he knew the cause of the young woman's discomfort.

He started into the bedroom but suddenly made a lightning decision. He wanted one more look at the case. Hastily he put on his coat and rushed out of the house. It mattered not at all that it was now two o'clock in the morning.

By this time hospital personnel had learned to accept the unexpected from Dr. Drew. Receptionists, office clerks, nurses, and most doctors liked him. He might be unpredictable, and exacting at times, but he was always fair. If he wanted to check something at an odd hour, that was up to him.

After he was given the patient's record, he studied it carefully and asked a few questions. Then he and the nurse gently woke the young woman. Surprised and sleepy, she answered his questions and grimaced as his probing fingers touched sensitive areas.

Dr. Drew smiled. "I have good news for you. I don't believe this's appendicitis, after all. We'll know for sure in the morning. How do you feel?"

"A little better," she admitted. "Guess the medicine you gave me last night helped. Oh, I do hope it means no operation!" Her eyes were pleading.

Dr. Drew knew she had been afraid. "We'll see," he said as he turned to leave.

She did not need the operation! His thoroughness in testing, probing, checking, and questioning the irregular symptom had saved expensive doctor and hospital fees and gained a patient's undying gratitude toward a determined and ethical physician.

Dr. Drew was happy in his work and in his home life, but things did not seem to be going well at his old home. Eva did not want to finish school. She often seemed wayward, a young

94

lady with a mind of her own. Mom was worried. She asked Charlie if he could do anything to help keep Eva in school.

Because of the growing demands of his own young family, it was harder now for Charlie to help his father's family. He promised to do what he could. For a while, however, he did not make much headway. There just was not time enough.

From one source and another, Dr. Drew had been receiving honors for his work with the plasma program and the first successful blood bank. Among the first was the E. S. Jones Award in 1943 for scientific research, from Tuskegee Institute.

In January of 1944, something else happened that made Dr. Drew happy. He felt it might have been due to his personal feelings, although he was never credited with this. The army withdrew its directive to keep bloods separated. The Subcommittee on Blood Substitutes of the National Research Council made a few changes in requirements for blood donors, and blood from all races was now accepted without qualification, and was not segregated! To Dr. Drew this was a real and necessary contribution to science. Both he and his wife quietly rejoiced.

Shortly afterward, on February 15, 1944, his third daughter, Rhea Sylvia, was born. If he were disappointed by another daughter, no one knew it. He welcomed her as he had the other two, played with her and watched her develop with the same keen enjoyment.

Then on July 16, 1944, another honor, the Spingarn medal, was bestowed upon him. This particular occasion greatly affected Eva.

Each year this medal is presented to the American Negro who has contributed most to black people as a race and to humankind as a whole. Certainly Dr. Drew's work in the blood bank and in the development of dried plasma, for Britain and later for the United States, was worthy of such recognition. In spite of this, Dr. Drew, fundamentally very humble, felt completely overwhelmed.

Although all members of his family wanted to be present for the presentation, only his wife, his mother, and his sister Eva were able to attend.

The day was hot, as only a day in Chicago can be, and the National Association for the Advancement of Colored People

(N.A.A.C.P.) convention was held at that time. Thousands of people, both black and white, were present. There were hot dogs, hamburgers, soda pop, and other refreshments. Music was played and speeches were made. Many friends and acquaintances wanted to see the Drews. Finally it was time for the presentation.

Walter White, national executive director of the N.A.A.C.P., put the wide gold and black ribbon with its simple medal over Dr. Drew's broad shoulders, then shook hands warmly.

As the bright medal, as large as the palm of his hand, with the words *For Merit* and a figure of Justice, dropped into place on his chest, Dr. Drew wished his father could be there. It had been almost ten years since Pop had been with them. How he would have liked the excitement—the people, the action, the color!

Dr. Drew thanked Mr. White and stepped before the microphone. Until this moment, he had not been sure what he wanted to say. Now as he stood before these thousands of people, he knew. His voice was not quite steady as he credited his parents for the splendid home life and direction they had given all their children.

"If I am what I am today, I have only my mother and father to thank. My mother, Mrs. Nora Drew—" He reached for her hand and pulled her up to stand beside him. She was a slight woman, her once-black hair now turning gray, and was obviously proud of her famous son. ". . . And my father, Richard Drew, who died in 1935. He was a strict man but just. Both my mother and my father took for granted that we'd get all the education we could. They knew it was the only way for us to get ahead. No children ever had finer parents."

He stopped, looked over the crowd, then went on. "But a man needs a wife, a helpmate to accompany him through life, helping in the ways only a wife can."

He drew Lenore to her feet. She stood tall and straight at his side, her black hair shining in the sun.

"And of course, little sisters to keep one on one's toes." He smiled as he beckoned for Eva to stand with them. She'd probably get even with him later, he thought, for calling her "little sister" before all these people.

Eva was no longer little. She was twenty-three—beautiful, tall, and golden blond—still trying to find herself.

It was not long after this that Eva returned to school. She always said it was to please her brother Charlie, but times were better now. She had attended Miner Teachers' College in Washington, D.C., from 1939 until 1943, but had not received a degree. Now, at his suggestion, she took Latin and French and English and also continued her painting; in 1945 she graduated with a B.A.

By now Dr. Drew had become chief-of-staff at Freedmen's Hospital, and he felt he could afford to send Eva to Italy to study art. She, however, had begun to think about joining some branch of the service, perhaps the WAVEs.

On May 8, 1945, Germany surrendered to the Allies, and on September 2, Japan surrendered. World War II was over, and Eva gave up the idea of entering the service. Instead, she began to teach first grade at Seaton School.

On October 30, 1945, one of the biggest events in Dr. Drew's personal life occurred—his son was born! Neither he nor his wife had thought much about a name for the new baby. Perhaps they both expected another girl. At any rate, by the time Mrs. Drew recovered enough to know what was happening around her, the baby had been named Charles Richard Drew, Junior.

A boy at last! What more could they want?

Twenty-two

Serving as a Trustee on Many Boards

DR. DREW CONTINUED TO RECEIVE AWARDS AND HONORS, and also took on many additional services. He was in great demand as a speaker for both lay and professional groups and conferences of various kinds. He became chairman of the surgical section of the National Medical Association and served on the executive board of the Twelfth Street branch of the Y.M.C.A., with which he had been associated in his boyhood.

In 1945 Dr. Drew received an honorary Doctor of Surgery degree from Virginia State College in Petersburg, Virginia, and in 1946 was elected a Fellow of the International College of Surgeons.

From 1946 until 1948, while he was medical director of Freedmen's Hospital in Washington, D.C., he served as trustee on a number of boards: the National Society for Crippled Children, the District of Columbia branch of the National Poliomyelitis Foundation, and the District of Columbia chapter of the American Cancer Society. He also served on the Dean's Committee of the Veterans Administration Hospital in Tuskegee, Alabama.

His energy seemed inexhaustible. He worked well under pressure, and in spite of the fact that his wife felt he should slow down, it seemed his drive to accomplish more and more would never cease.

In June of 1947, Charles Cole, president of Charlie Drew's alma mater Amherst College, felt honored to give its former student an honorary Doctor of Science degree. He commented on Dr. Drew's brilliant career, both in athletics and in medicine, and the fact that he had written many articles and books in the scientific field.

In that same year Charlie had one more service to perform for his father's family. He gave "baby" sister Eva away in marriage to Phillip Johnson, a graduate of Howard University, with a master's degree in psychology. It was a charming wedding, performed in sister Nora's home on April 3, a cool spring day. All members of the family were present.

It was a happy marriage, but it was soon saddened. The young husband developed multiple sclerosis. Neither Dr. Drew nor other doctors, with all their medical knowledge, could prevent the wasting away of the muscles in this devastating disease. The doctor felt as much frustration at his helplessness as he had when his father died.

His sister Elsie's death many years previously had sparked Charlie Drew's first desire for medical knowledge. He had been able to help save thousands of lives, but could do nothing to save loved ones in his own family. What a lot was yet to be learned!

Phillip Johnson died twelve years later, having spent six of those years in a hospital. Members of the family did all they could to ease Eva's pain, but they knew there are certain things in life that only time can dim. Grief is one of those things.

Freedmen's, under Dr. Drew's capable direction, was fast becoming outstanding in the surgical training of young Negroes. He went out of his way to instill confidence in his students. In the operating room, he insisted, technical matters should be behind them; there, confidence and ability were vital. Good surgeons did not panic under stress.

Dr. Drew himself set a good example. Dr. Mordecai Johnson, then president of Howard, said that Dr. Drew had an extraordinary capacity to organize himself completely for the attainment of his goals. And he tried to teach this talent for organization to his students.

He felt his life would be a success if he could train twenty top surgeons who could be a credit to their race and profession. To him this was far more important than a private practice. He was proud of the five young men who had already achieved this goal and were doing well in their profession. He only needed time to train the other fifteen.

In 1949 Dr. Drew lectured on "Negro Scholars in Scientific Research" at the annual meeting in New York City of the Association for the Study of Negro Life and History. Also during that year, on his first "vacation," he and five other doctors toured hospital installations in occupied Europe. Dr. Drew served as surgical consultant to the surgeon general of the army; the group's mission was to improve the quality of medical care and instruction in the various installations.

Seeing Europe in the aftermath of war, he could only visualize the horror and destruction that had occurred. It gave him a sense of humility and deep satisfaction to know that he had had such a vital part in helping to save lives during that time.

The year of 1950 began as work-filled as all his previous years. His burning passion to help make a better world would not allow him to slow down for a moment.

He felt more strongly than ever that surgeons had the responsibility to pass their knowledge on to the next generation. He was not interested in making big money; his salary from Howard was quite adequate. He was interested only in human beings—especially young Negroes—and their talents.

Twenty-three

Dr. Drew Dies Tragically in 1950

FRIDAY, MARCH 31, 1950, HAD BEEN AN UNUSUALLY BUSY DAY for Dr. Drew. Lenore was right. He *should* slow down! Rest, however, could wait until after tomorrow's trip—too many things still to be done, too many loose ends to be tied up before tonight's meeting.

Tomorrow in Tuskegee, he would speak before the John Andrew Clinical Society. He really should arrange his time to have a day of rest before attempting that long trip each year. Perhaps next year he could manage differently. Meetings, meetings—just too many meetings, and they all took time.

Perhaps next week he and Lenore and the children could do something to make up for his absence from home lately. That son . . . Dr. Drew smiled happily whenever he thought of his children, especially his four-year-old son. A fine little lad. Maybe he'd follow in his old dad's footsteps and become a doctor. A lot of work—yes, a lot of hard study to prepare for such a career—but a lot of satisfaction. No finer career in the world. Dr. Drew shook his head. This was no time to daydream; he had work to do, and he was tired. As Friday drew to a close he wished tonight's meeting had not been scheduled. It meant they would get a late start on their trip.

He and three young doctors, Walter Johnson, John Ford, and Samuel Bullock, had decided to drive, although originally he had planned to go by train. The young fellows did not have much money so he had decided to help them in this way: they could share expenses, and since they would be taking turns at the wheel, it should not be too bad.

When Dr. Drew finished his long evening, he dashed home to change and pick up his bag. By the time he was ready to leave, it was two o'clock in the morning on April 1—a cool, crisp morning that promised good driving. He had yet to pick up the other three doctors.

Mrs. Drew knew she could not talk him out of starting at this awful hour, although she did mention to him that he looked tired.

Jokingly he said, "Now, Lenore, you know this old body is good for a long time yet. I'll rest up when I get home. That's a promise!" He kissed her good-bye. "Tell the children good-bye for me. I'll see all of you Sunday."

As he crossed the yard to the garage, his bag swinging, Mrs. Drew watched from the porch. She bit her lip thoughtfully. If only he didn't work so hard. He was such a wonderful man, such a kind father, such a good husband. He should have gone by train, so he could rest on the way. Some day when the children were grown, perhaps she could take these trips with him. They had often discussed this and looked forward to it.

That was the last time Mrs. Drew saw her husband alive.

Shortly after eight o'clock the next morning, there was a knock on her door. She was startled to see four of their doctor friends standing before her.

She caught her breath. "Charlie! Something's happened to Charlie!"

Burke Syphax nodded slowly. "Yes." He tried to speak gently. "Their car turned over near Burlington, North Carolina. Charlie's dead."

Mrs. Drew was numb. She hardly heard his words or felt the kind arm of Lillian Wheeler around her. It was as though she had no control over what was happening to her.

Dr. Wheeler went to break the terrible news to the children, while Dr. Syphax, Robert Jason, and Clarence Green

104

gave Mrs. Drew as much information as they had about the accident. When the car turned over, Dr. Drew had been crushed behind the wheel. Dr. Ford had a broken arm and cuts; the other two doctors were only slightly injured.

Everything was done that could have been done to save Dr. Drew. Ambulance service was prompt; medical care, including use of plasma, was excellent; but the crushed chest could not respond.

No one knew whether a heart attack had caused the accident or he had gone to sleep at the wheel. Mrs. Drew kept remembering he had said he was tired.

Charlie Drew had been a sprinter in life, but the magnificent body was resting at last, just two months before his forty-sixth birthday.

His family and his students and colleagues, as well as the entire medical profession and scientific world, would miss him. But though his time on earth was over, his work would live on in the hands of his many dedicated students. In addition to his splendid research in blood and blood plasma which saved thousands of lives—not only during war but for the civilian population since the 1940s—Dr. Charles Richard Drew's greatest achievement was turning out superbly qualified surgeons. In fact, two-thirds of the black surgeons in the United States at that time had trained under him at Howard.

Yes, his work lives on, in many ways, through the lives of others.

Now, forty-one years later, the question still arises, Did Dr. Drew have good care at the time of the accident? There is much evidence to support the belief that Charles Drew received the very best of care. Dr. Charles Mason Quick, a black physician in Fayetteville, North Carolina, arrived at Alamance General Hospital the day of the accident to see white doctors working desperately to save the life of his friend Charles Drew. The doctors knew the latter only as a black man who had been injured in an automobile accident. Dr. Quick watched them do everything they could, including trying to give him a blood transfusion, which was available. His chest had been crushed, making their efforts futile.

"The deep South can be blamed for a number of things but not his death. Charlie never had a chance to be admitted to the general hospital because he *died in emergency*," Dr. Quick adamantly stated.

Marvin E. Yount, Jr., a white man, now administrator of Memorial Hospital of Alamance County in Burlington, remembers well when Dr. Drew was brought to old Alamance General, the only hospital available at that time. He was on duty that day.

Dr. Drew was not denied care of any kind, but "received some of the best treatment we had," Yount verified to the American Red Cross when inquiry was made.

A letter from Lenore Drew in Alamance General Hospital's files states, "Though all efforts were futile, there is much comfort derived from knowing that everything was done in his fight for life."

EPILOGUE

In addition to the institutions Dr. Charles R. Drew helped shape as a trustee, and the many public schools all over the country named after him posthumously, his memory lives on in the honors which are still being bestowed upon him.

In 1977, the Charles Richard Drew House, present home of brother Joseph L. Drew and his wife, Grace, in Arlington, Virginia, was designated a National Historic Landmark and was placed on the Virginia Landmark Register. This house has been in the Drew family since 1920, when it was purchased by Richard and Nora Drew, Charlie's parents. Many of the lovely trees and shrubs were planted by Charlie and his brother Joe, with their father supervising. It was a happy home, replacing the one in Foggy Bottom, at our nation's capital, where their sister Elsie had died in 1918 during a relentless influenza epidemic.

On June 3, 1981, the 77th anniversary of his birth, a ceremony was held at the Howard University Hospital honoring Dr. Drew on the occasion of the first day of issue of a new thirty-five-cent stamp honoring him. This was the third stamp in the Great American series. A large, enthusiastic audience witnessed this impressive ceremony. The program ended with the words, "Postage stamps are powerful communicators, which can remind millions of people throughout the nation and the world of the outstanding accomplishments of this truly Great American."

On Saturday, April 5, 1986, on the stretch of NC 49 north of Haw River, near Burlington, North Carolina, almost four hundred citizens, officials, Omega Psi Phi fraternity members, and Drew family members attended a ceremony which showed deep respect and love for this highly dedicated man. A bronze plaque listing his accomplishments was bolted onto a six-foot granite marker. The monument extols Dr. Drew as a scientist in the field of blood transfusions, director of the first American Red Cross Blood Bank, mentor and teacher to a generation of American doctors, outstanding athlete, and foe of racial injustice. Charlene Drew Jarvis, the second of Dr. Drew's three daughters and a councilwoman in Washington, D.C., unveiled the marker.